Treasure of Victoria Peak

Phil A. Koury

West Chester, Pennsylvania

Doc Noss atop "Blackie" with his dog "Buster". This photo was taken in 1941.

Also by Phil A. Koury
Yes, Mr. DeMille (G.P. Putnam's Sons)
Two Reels and a Crank (Doubleday)
Stover: An American Success Story (Random House)
The 64 Days (mms.)

Printed in the United States of America.
ISBN: 0-88740-060-4
Published by Schiffer Publishing Ltd., 1469 Morstein Road, West Chester, Pennsylvania 19380
This book may be purchased from the publisher.
Please include $1.50 postage.
Try your bookstore first.

Author's Note

For much that is in these pages, I have relied upon personal experience and observation, supported bountifully by files accumulated during the decade and a half I was legal counsel to the story's central figure, Ova Noss, wife of Milton E. (Doc) Noss at the time of his astonishing discovery at Victoria Peak.

Also, the records and files of several state and federal government offices have been most helpful, notably the New Mexico Land Office in Santa Fe and the Department of the Army. To a lesser extent, because its involvement was minimal and sporadic, the U. S. Treasury department yielded important data.

Nothing herein was entrusted to conjecture, a stratagem so often employed in lost-gold legends. With its contemporary setting, its living and, in many instances, well-known participants, the Noss story has little or no need of artifice or invention. It came to involve persons in high places, secular and official, and directly challenged a number of judicial, military and political agencies. All in all, one salient fact of its history calls out for affirmation — the largest land treasure of its kind ever found in America.

P. K.

Victoria Peak—The winding road leads to the summit and the original shaft-entry leading to the treasure rooms.

A view of Victoria Peak from Hembrillo Basin.

Contents

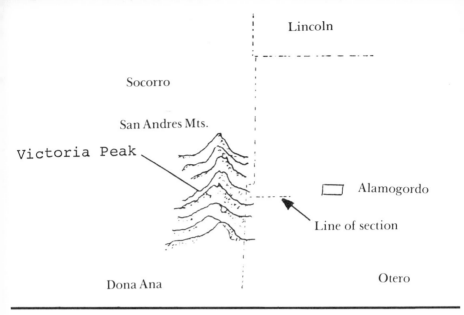

Index map of Southwestern New Mexico

The man who found the treasure, M. E. Noss.

The finding

Hembrillo basin is ugly and rude. Winds and rain have creased the ground and the footing is perilous. Spiny, deep-rooted shrubs and an occasional cluster of hackberry and pinon invest the rugged slopes, especially where the valley is deep. In the basin's center rises Victoria Peak, north and east of the town of Hatch, New Mexico, and almost due north of Las Cruces. Its jagged fingers of rock resemble inverted stalactites, a pipe-organ-like formation some 400 feet high at the southern tip of the San Andres.

Doc Noss stood at the foot of one of the faulted hills that rise unevenly from the rutted canyon floor. He was there to hunt the area but more in response to his love of a region that once was home to Indian tribes and such brave chieftains as Victorio, alleged namesake of Victoria Peak.

His eye, trained by experience to such calculations, trailed past visible evidences of thin shale beds. At the summit a dark greenish overlay changed to massive pale ledges of limestone.

As he peered up, shading his eyes from the sun, he saw the familiar gaping cleavage, as if a mighty ax had laid open the peak's brow. Such crevices are not unusual along the San Andres, shaped by erosive wind and rain, offering refuge to animal life and sun-shy flora. And, even more providentially, vaults for the secrets of early explorers and Spanish conquistadors.

With a firm grasp on his hunting rifle, he picked his way up the ridges and loose shale. At the summit he scanned the region from two or three directions for a stray deer, his special quarry on such meanderings. Then sat down to rest. He was not far from the dike-like formation that bisected the hill and ran for several miles in an easterly direction, a wide breach prominently exposed for a considerable distance.

He was picking up shale pebbles and tossing them idly toward a crevice.

As he sat there resting, his attention was drawn to a thick rock overhang, protruding far enough out from the peak to protect from wind and rain the space beneath it. Curious as to whether there was actually a cavern there, or perhaps an entry to one, he lowered himself gingerly into a crevice, steadied himself by probing for indentations in the uneven wall of the crevice and, some twenty feet below the point from which he began the descent, entered a room-like formation. Intuitively he knew it had been a shelter, possibly for periods longer than an overnight refuge.

He reached down, brushed loose the earth at the perimeter of a flat round stone near the center of the cave. Unable to lift or move it to one side he scraped away more dirt that gripped its edges. As the stone yielded slowly, a deep shaft came into his view and an upward burst of an unpleasant musty odor assaulted his nostrils.

His sensibilities were at full alert — an instinctive reaction of prospectors experienced in detecting and analyzing odors that rise from great crevices in the earth. It was a bad odor, probably from dry guano deposited by bats, causing him to conclude there might be a large cavern or cave quite near.

He peered down the shaft-like crevice, reflected on its depth and size. He guessed it might be large enough at deeper levels to accommodate him. Even with the afternoon sun he was not able to see more than a few feet into its depths.

As far as he could tell, its walls were earthen and fairly

smooth, though he observed rocky protrusions here and there that might provide reasonably secure footholds. With these and a few visible outcrops he could try to pick his way down into the shaft.

But not that day.

Nearing 5 o'clock, it would soon be too dark to permit even a cursory probe.

Whatever his feelings — excitement, perhaps even a sudden impulse to fantasy — he could not envision the ultimate outcome, how the events of that day in the San Andres mountains, at Section 16, Township 16S, Range 3E, State of New Mexico, County of Dona Ana, would push him into circumstances of violence and tragedy.

The following day, with what little money he had, Noss purchased a few items — a flashlight, rope and a large over-the-shoulder canvas bag. On the second day he probed for footholds in the rough places of the almost vertical shaft wall. Carefully straddling it he lowered himself into the darkness. An hour of slow exploration left him exhausted. He had not reached the bottom of the shaft and was unable to determine its depth. The descent was slow and dangerous with only earthen ledges as supports, requiring great care in each step to test their strength. He knew he would need better equipment, and much stronger lighting.

Time was not vital. Several weeks passed, punctuated by trips to the peak. He did not attempt a probe at each visit, sitting on the floor at the shaft-point of entry and speculating on whether he was caught up in a fruitless endeavor. His calculations pointed, not to a single shaft, but a series of shaft-like crevices, each leading off into a slightly different direction, so at times the descent would not be entirely vertical. It might take weeks, he guessed, to penetrate the lower reaches of the peak.

The treasures

To a shrewd practitioner like Milton Ernest Noss, adversity had its special opportunities. Wisely used, they could be profitable. At one stage in his life, for reasons that a somewhat hazy record does not make clear, Noss took to foot doctoring. He had no schooling in the art. Nor did he bother about such requirements as a license or medical society affiliation.

His clientele chiefly were herdsmen and prospectors, their extremities ravaged by long trips over rough terrain and needing the kind of practical chiropody of which the quiet "medic" was capable. They were intrigued by his knowledge of the country, and it is likely the shop talk helped draw their attention away from his coarse and clumsy methods. They thanked "Doc", paid him for the visit with a few coins or a gold-tinged hunk of ore, and waved as they left, bright-eyed with anticipation, on another arduous trek into the mountains. He kept office hours only long enough to replenish his treasury, and like his peers took off toward the grey hills on missions inspired by rumor or the fantasies of a grizzled prospector ever on the verge of an important find.

Noss was undeniably handsome, tall and trim of waist with jet black hair. Though two-thirds Cheyenne, his light skin and regular features almost totally concealed a predominantly Indian heritage. He spoke Spanish capably and was fluent in the language of several Indian tribes. He found it easy to inspire confidence, a facility that brought him face to face with all sorts of temptation. Unfortunately a concealed yet intense hatred of whites was itself sufficient to influence his judgments.

The opaqueness of the chill dark turned the distant hills into shadowy, sullen ghosts. In the early predawn hours he had followed an ill-kept narrow gravel road that became a footpath as he moved onto the basin floor. Soon there was a beginning sun.

He had brought a much larger battery-type lantern. His movements were infinitely deliberate as he put himself into the shaft, first feeling the cold damp walls for niches to steady the descent by bracing himself against an opposite wall. The light of the sun was able to produce a faint grayness only in the upper reaches of the shaft.

He knew it would be hours before he returned; the climb up the shaft would drain him of much of his strength. After hours of slow, deliberate effort he reached the bottom of the shaft. He guessed he had gone 150 feet in a somewhat less than vertical direction. Next, he squeezed through an opening almost too small to admit him. He found himself standing in a corridor-like formation. He moved forward cautiously perhaps a dozen strides, at this point detecting the sound of rushing water. He paused, the thin finger of light from his lantern barely penetrating the darkness to the other bank. It was too great a distance to step or leap across. Nor was he certain of the stream's depth. The enveloping dark and dampness began to pall on him as he remembered the tortuous climb back up the shaft. He retreated, deciding to attempt a fording another day.

The very existence of the stream added to his excitement. He knew how vital water was in a mining operation. Suddenly he recalled seeing a small stone structure, long since abandoned, at the southeast foot of the peak.

Possibilities flooded his mind . . .

Was he moving toward quarters that once served early *vaqueros* seeking safety from Indian attacks?

Was the shaft an air vent for the smelting of copper or silver, both geologically abundant in the area?

Was there an entrance, nestled somewhere under a burden of earth and rock, leading to a depository for treasures of the type which legends trace to 16th century conquistadors?

He knew enough of local history to remember the bloody Indian wars that led to the nadir of the American Indian. Many lives were lost and great treasure hordes vanished. Tribes had come from the north to escape the cold and hunger. Others drifted in from the east, where the senseless forays of white marauders had made life intolerable. The impact of these migrations provoked seventy years of war for control of the West, a conflict that spread across the plains into Texas and Old Mexico through the New Mexico and Arizona territories.

Superb figures emerged. None more cruel or resourceful than the Apache chief Victorio. Later, other Apache greats like Geronimo and Cochise would appear but it was Victorio who terrorized the countryside, raiding and burning until at the turn of the century he was run to earth deep in Mexico.

Now he would attempt to cross the stream, probing the water at each step with a long pole. On this occasion his wife, Ova, was with him and watched him disappear into the shaft. She built a fire a few feet from the edge of the shaft and awaited his return. An hour passed, then another. She stoked the fire and began to prepare a meal.

It was near dusk when he appeared, grimy and gasping for breath, his eyes wide with excitement. The shoulder strap on the canvas bag was taut with the weight of the contents. He placed it on the ground and slowly lifted the bottom to shunt the contents toward the mouth of the bag, without spilling them on the ground. It was half full of trinkets — medals of a religious type and a number of silver articles. He said he had taken them from a casket in one of several natural caverns. He held up a blackened bar, probably iron or an iron ore, then tossed it to the ground a few feet from the fire.

He told her what he had seen: several caverns opening off a long corridor that ran some 1,000 feet from the base of the shaft to the caverns deep into the belly of the peak. In one of the rooms he saw two huge stacks of heavy bars, like the one he had brought with him. There was a third smaller stack and some chests with the words "Silver Bullion" marked on them. In another room were church garments, religious books, swords and statues of religious figures.

Both made an effort to restrain their excitement over the discovery. He told her that their secret must not be revealed. He spoke quietly of various moves he would make later but, for now, not a word to anyone.

As he sat on the ground, resting, his attention was drawn to a reflection of light emanating from near the campfire. He walked over, picked up the bar and saw that it had been scratched where it had struck the ground. He scraped the side of the bar with a knife, then pushed a thumb into the soft ore.

Slowly he carved off a chip, gazed at it in stunned silence as thoughts raced through his mind struggling to accept the awesome reality of the moment.

A single, hushed word escaped his lips:

"Gold!"

Suspicious always, he was now suddenly and acutely conscious of the burden of his discovery. He knew gold mining was not common to the area and doubted that the gold bars he had found had been mined in the caverns. Should he make inquiries at the State minerals office in Santa Fe? Should he apply for a permit? Should he chance disclosure or some sort of legal move? No, none of these. The risks were too great. For the time being it would be better to remove as much of the gold as possible, and hide it.

He reflected on, then rejected, the significance of

something else he had seen in one of the rooms — a small underground Spanish smelter comprising two bull-hide bellows, vassos, ingot molds, and a stack of mountain mahogany probably used as fuel.

Over the years there were many rumors and much speculation about a "lost" gold mine in the San Andres region.

The most widely publicized was an account involving a Spanish priest named LaRue, stationed at a hacienda in Chihuahua in the late years of the Spanish occupation of New Mexico. According to the legend, a man gravely ill told Father LaRue about a gold-bearing lode located in mountains some two days' journey north of Paso del Norte. Father LaRue listened intently and tucked the details into his memory.

Shortly thereafter a drought and famine plagued the community of peons in his charge at the hacienda. He persuaded them to migrate northward with him to the San Andres mountains. Once there, the priest recognized landmarks which his dying friend had described. With two trustworthy friends, he searched the area and in time succeeded in locating the rich deposits. The colony settled at what was then Spirit Springs and there the gold was concentrated in arrastres. Some of the ore was smelted in *vassos* (adobe furnaces). The legend places the mine in a canyon southwest of Spirit Springs.

Father LaRue was much too busy to send a message back to his superiors. His long silence caused apprehension among the ecclesiastics in Mexico City, and a small military force to find him was dispatched to LaRue's first place of labor. Finding it deserted, the soldiers traced him to the general vicinity of the San Andres. Informed that soldiers were in the area, Father LaRue ordered the mine covered and the gold hidden. When the expedition arrived, the priest refused to divulge the whereabouts of the gold, asserting the treasure belonged to his people, not to the Church. Violent arguments led to threats and one night the priest was murdered and his followers dispersed. The soldiers began a frantic search for clues that would lead them to the treasure. The effort was futile; only the priest and a handful of aides knew the exact location.

Indications of early habitation have been found in the area, mostly remains of an ancient Indian camp. In a canyon near Victoria Peak, Indian shards and metates were uncovered as recently as two decades ago. Historians have surmised that the inhabitants of the camp might have been workers brought by the early Spanish padre to help at the mine. While the records, scanty as they are, do not affirm or deny that the LaRue cache and the Noss trove are one and the same, it is unlikely there could exist simultaneously two such sizable treasures in the same general area.

"Doc" and Ova moved into the stone house at the foot of the peak, going about their tasks as inconspicuously as possible. They remained indoors through most of the daylight hours and kept to a minimum errands for food and firewood. As a precaution it was his habit to descend into the shaft late in the day.

An incident occurred which deepened their fear that even the slightest news of the discovery would bring a swift end to their secret.

Noss had decided to show the first gold bar to a friend, Henry Lard, a banker in Hot Springs.

Lard, startled by the sight, asked where he had found it.

Noss hesitated.

"In the Caballo mountains?"

"That's right," replied Noss, aware that the Caballos were miles from Victoria Peak.

Within a few days the Caballos became the scene of a major gold rush, encampments dotting the mountainside like mushrooms. Noss' falsehood had spread swiftly.

Still, the experience with the banker did not lessen his

determination to sell some of his gold.

But how to do it without risk?

The dilemma preyed on his mind for weeks. He wondered whether it would be better to leave the treasure where it was, secure in the inner recesses of the peak, or sell it to contacts in face-to-face exchanges. He was not oblivious to the possibility of violence at the hands of racketeers and transients once his secret became known.

It was just as well that the circumstances did not call for immediate removal of the treasures. The sheer physical task of hauling only a few bars to the surface would have been too great for one person. Durable as he was, he could not manage more than a single journey a week. The trip from the base of the peak to the top was not itself a small feat.

Two bars, each weighing about thirty pounds, were his maximum load on any single climb to the surface, though now and then he would include a third item in the canvas bag, usually an artifact of modest size.

At one point he brought up an old, decoratively engraved Spanish sword and later a silver bowl. (I was shown the sword by Mrs. Noss years later in her mobile home in Clovis.)

Noss divulged little about the treasures in the caverns, even to his wife. Only an occasional exuberant comment over a find that struck his fancy.

Nonetheless, Ova made notes of these various disclosures, thus was able to compile a kind of inventory. She felt there was much more in the caves than she was able to extract from the comments of her evasive husband.

One day she produced a list which she had compiled in this manner. It included:

Stacks of gold bars,
swords and daggers,
gold statues and candlesticks,
bags of ancient coins,

stone jars of uncut gems, in ore form,
chests inscribed "Silver",
silver and gold goblets,
trunks of religious clothing,
religious altar and furniture,
scrolls.

Not unexpectedly, a change came over Noss. He brooded over the fact there seemed no way out of his dilemma. If he made known his discovery, or if he did not, he was in violation of laws that made possession of gold bullion illegal. Either way, he thought, he was in for it.

As time went on, there was less and less conversation with Mrs. Noss. Communication went to matters only of existence, like daily chores, food or clothing. He moved about furtively at night and refused to tell her where he had been or what he was doing. On occasions of his return from the caverns, he would disappear into the night with varied items, hiding them in places away from the usual paths of hunters and prospectors. He would stroll off quietly on other nights, presumably to check on a hidden cache or mark off new and better places of concealment.

Part of his strategy was to return to their home in Hot Springs (now Truth and Consequences) occasionally to allay the curiosity of neighbors and friends. And also to scratch about for more funds. Ova waited tables during these interim periods, and he would open his office to an occasional patient with foot problems.

It was on one of the visits to town that Noss made his second disclosure of the existence of the treasure. The listener, smiling, agreed to pay a modest sum for a bar of gold once satisfied that it indeed was gold. Noss did not follow up on the opportunity. He knew he could not ask for even a reasonable price — let alone the fair value of a bar of gold.

Perhaps, he reasoned, he could dispose of a part of a bar. With this in mind, he bought a small vise and set it up near the foot of the peak, not far from the stone house. He was at the vise one morning when he heard footsteps, and turning saw a young man walking toward him.

The stranger said his name was Joe Andregg, that he was helping his father on a farm across the way, pointing to the east, and would like part-time work. They chatted for a few minutes, Noss being careful to explain he was doing a little prospecting and probably could use some help for a few days for the next week or so, and maybe more later on.

Gradually, Noss took a liking to the 15-year-old. After a week or two he made no effort to conceal the nature of his find and Andregg soon was aware that his employer had indeed found gold. How much, however, he had no idea.

One day Noss placed a gold bar in the vise, sawed off small pieces, placed them in a rough cloth sack, and invited Andregg to join him in an old pickup truck, which Noss had borrowed from a friend, and drove to El Paso. There Noss went off alone, bag in hand, to peddle the gold, presumably to contacts with whom he must have made previous arrangements.

The excited reaction from the banker Lard had convinced Noss he could not use ordinary channels in disposing of the gold. Yet, he needed a fairly substantial amount of money for two projects at the peak — one to facilitate his entry into the access tunnel leading to the treasures, the other to construct some kind of a roadway from the base of the peak to the top. As it was, he was carting heavy loads of gold at night down steep, rutted terrain.

Several months after the bank episode Noss appeared at the U. S. Mint in Denver, carrying three gold bars wrapped in ordinary brown store paper. He handed the package to a clerk and said he wanted to sell the gold to the mint. The amazed clerk disappeared and quickly returned with a supervisor who took possession of the bars "for examination" and disappeared into another office. After a considerable period he reappeared, told Noss that the bars were of a very high gold content and asked where he had got them.

Noss said he could not give that information, and continued to refuse in the face of the supervisor's insistence that Noss had no other choice, inasmuch as it was not legal to possess gold bullion.

Now, acutely aware that the mission was a serious mistake and fearful of arrest, Noss asked the supervisor to give him back his gold and he would be on his way. Instead, the supervisor handed him a receipt designating the Denver mint as the issuer and stating that M. E. Noss had deposited gold bullion with a value in excess of $90,000. Fearful of arrest, Noss accepted it and moving quickly toward the exit heard the supervisor say that the government would hold the gold until he returned with proper proof of ownership.

Months later, Noss revealed to Ova a few details of the trip. He told her he had put the receipt in a strong box, along with other valuables, and hid it not far from Victoria Peak. Years after his death, Ova went to the Denver mint and attempted to obtain a copy of the receipt, only to be told the records did not disclose anyone had visited the mint by the name of M. E. Noss, or that a receipt for gold was given to such a person. (In 1962, I also visited the mint to verify the fact of Noss' appearance there, but received the same reply.)

Persons outside the Noss family, myself included, looked upon the receipt as a sort of single-instrument verification of the existence of the treasure trove and an affirmation of the truth of Noss's claims. Mrs. Noss was certain the receipt would show up one day.

The dynamiting

For Noss, a good part of the physical hardship involved in retrieving the gold took place at the bottom of the shaft. On every visit he was forced to squeeze through a hole rimmed with jagged rock in order to reach the access tunnel. He would burrow painfully through a space not quite large enough to accommodate his trim shoulders. He accomplished the feat inch by inch at the cost often of torn clothes and body welts. He was able to speed his movements up and down the shaft with the aid of heavy rope and later a pulley, but the passage through the hole was intolerably difficult. He remarked often to Ova and the youth Andregg that something had to be done about the opening. It must be widened; items in the treasure rooms, including several chests, were too large to pass through it.

Of all the consequences of his acts — rash and improvident as many were — his next move triggered the most far-reaching.

It took place in 1939, about two years after the discovery. In itself, the plan was reasonable — a small charge of dynamite carefully placed would most certainly splinter the nubs of hard rock and thus enlarge the opening.

Noss contacted a C. E. Montgomery, reputed to be skilled in the use and effects of dynamite. With Noss at his side Montgomery set a charge at the bottom of the shaft. When both were safely out of and beyond the mouth of the shaft, Montgomery touched it off.

At that moment Mrs. Noss was doing a housekeeping

chore near the stone house. Andregg was busy at the foot of the peak but at some distance from the house.

Both heard a muffled boom of considerable intensity. They saw dirt and debris spray upward, showering down on Noss and Montgomery.

Ova recalled, "The next thing I saw was Doc chasing that fella down the hill. He had taken off one boot and he was so angry I know he would have beat him to death with it if he could have caught up with him."

Noss' unshod foot was torn and bleeding by the time the chase reached the base of the hill, thus expediting Montgomery's escape across the basin.

It was a calamity. Whether excessive or its directional force miscalculated, the dynamite caused a total collapse throughout the entire length of the 200-foot shaft.

The treasures were effectively sealed off.

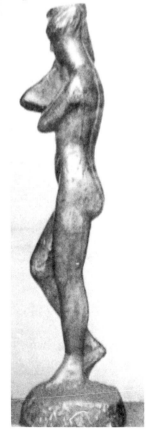

Noss, wife of the founder, says this is a photo of bars of gold which Doc Noss removed from ria Peak in the late '30's and hid them in ter location—from an article in the Albuquer-Tribune, August 10, 1973.

is the gold statue removed by Doc Noss from the re room. While its ultimate disposition remains tery, there is evidence that he sold it for a few red dollars in a secret negotiation in El Paso,

The keepers

In the art of examining witnesses, lawyers make use of what is frequently known in the profession as the rule of reason — testing the behavior of the witness on the basis of common sense and ordinary experience, observing the manner of his response to a particular set of inquiries.

At many points the Noss story seems to reject the test of plausibility. Its contradictions, factual conflicts and paradoxes in human behavior invite reactions of suspicion and disbelief.

Over a period of sixteen years my research of the Noss documents and visits with persons directly and marginally involved did produce a rather confused and uneven record. Alone, the fact is not surprising. Gold is the eternal dream, by its nature conducive to secrecy, deception and conspiracy, often a struggle between the finder determined to protect his treasure at any cost and outsiders equally intent on acquiring it, often by stealth or violence.

In his journey to the caverns Noss had emerged with enough gold bars to constitute a sizable treasure. So even after the collapse of the shaft he continued his efforts to sell chunks of the metal. Some of these negotiations took surprising turns. Noss was cautious and ever suspicious, always on the alert for signs of betrayal, even on the part of those who seemed intent on being helpful.

When he decided someone was trying to cheat or outmaneuver him he resorted to an unusual strategy. On the day of the encounter, Noss would appear, not with a bar but with an ordinary brick painted a golden color. Feigning a desire for fair play, he would suggest that the brick be carefully examined before payment is made. Whereupon the other party, observing the phony bar, would beat a hasty and often angry retreat; thus the would-be deceiver was routed without serious complications.

As a result, naturally, word got around that Doc Noss was trying to peddle painted bricks.

Such strategy on Noss' part may explain his numerous brushes with the law, mostly for disturbances of the peace. The records, however, reveal no conviction for fraudulent sales; he was able to satisfy law enforcement officers that his sole purpose was to protect himself from crooks and confidence men.

There was an even more tantalizing aspect — the civil law's attitude toward his discovery. He employed devious and elaborate efforts to stay beyond what he felt was the outstretched arm of the law, a vigilant enemy seeking to seize him and his treasure. Had he consulted anyone familiar with the cases on treasure trove he would have learned that the law was solidly on his side. By the great weight of legal authorities he could have safely announced his discovery to the authorities and his rights would have been protected. His entitlement to the gold would have been good against all the world except, as the cases put it, the true owner — the party who placed it there originally, a party not identifiable in the Noss case.

After the collapse of the shaft, Noss' feelings were not unlike those of a gambler who had won handsomely at the table and was not allowed to cart home his gains. Still, he was very much ahead of the game. His personal worth in gold in-hand was substantial; his equity in gold out-of-hand would gladden the heart of the greediest. True, his cash flow at the moment was not particularly good but, for that matter, it had never been very steady. If fate were forcing him to an extreme — of disposing of the gold piece by piece, well, so be it.

He felt a glow of satisfaction as he reflected on what had been accomplished as a result of his labors at the peak, back-breaking though they were. He had removed several hundred gold bars from the cavern, hid them in pockets and crevices in the immediate vicinity. He was aware of the habits of ardent rock and gem hounds who were wont to probe about in the area; the places he chose to conceal the bars were well removed from such popular hunting grounds.

It was his estimate that more than 16,000 bars of gold were still stacked on ricks in the caverns, and there they would remain. For how long, no one knew. Meanwhile, he felt he could live well on the gold brought to the surface, thus, scratching good out of misfortune. He realized the blast had eliminated one worry — that someone might find the shaft and enter the caverns. On rare occasions, as he set about the task of finding buyers for the gold, in whole bars or smaller pieces, he communicated to others the facts of his discovery and predicament, and solicited their suggestions. Quickly, he encountered offers of service or physical help. He gave a large gold medallion to an attorney in return for legal assistance in the event of arrest. The attorney gazed at the medallion and exclaimed, "This will buy half the city of El Paso!"

In this period his principal aim was to find a person or persons interested in buying a percentage of his equity in order to accumulate enough cash to buy the necessary equipment with which to excavate and reopen the shaft. As time went on, he gave a number of small percentages to various individuals with political influence in the hope they might be helpful in the future. Most important, however, were the initial contracts — dollars in exchange for a contingent interest in the Victoria Peak enterprise.

Records at the State Land Office in Santa Fe indicate Noss entered into numerous and varied arrangements.

Many of the claims are evidenced by affidavits, citing an outright transfer or assignment of a percentage of the Noss' interest in the treasure. Some involved as little as one-twentieth of one percent, frequently given on the assurance the recipient would help obtain "front money" from other individuals. In a few instances persons with small percentages transferred a part or all of their claim to third parties.

One day Noss invited an engineer consultant, a Gordon E. Herkenhoff of Albuquerque, to invest in his venture. The engineer said he might be interested, but first would like to see something of value from one of the caverns. Noss produced a gold brick which Herkenhoff inspected with an intensity appropriate to the occasion. The engineer did not express a judgment, except to say he was not interested in any arrangement. But several years later, in 1946, Herkenhoff was hired by the State of New Mexico to investigate and report on the Noss family claims because, at the time, Noss was asking the state office for three separate permits to conduct mining operations in the Hembrillo basin.

According to Herkenhoff's report on file in the Santa Fe Land Office he met Noss in Hot Springs in early February and spent the day going over background and historical details with him. "Noss told me he had entered the mine through a cave, had seen the gold and other treasures contained therein, and when he was ready to remove the gold, a cave-in some 186 feet down the entrance shaft sealed the entrance and nothing further has been done to gain entrance to the mine."

In his inspection of the workings Herkenhoff found that some work had been done on what he described as "the Big Fault No. 1 claim." His report continues: "This claim has on it a shaft which is supposed to be the opening for getting into the treasure cave. The shaft is approximately 6 feet x 6 feet square, timbered to a depth of approximately 60 feet. The shaft is reported to be 186 feet deep, with no timber beyond the 60-foot mark. I could not gain entrance to the shaft for lack of proper equipment to go beyond the timbered section. Noss claims that beyond the 186-foot depth, there is an incline downward at 45 degrees for 72 feet, which is now plugged by the cave-in. Beyond that, there is supposed to be another incline upward at about 30 degrees for some short distance (40 feet as I remember it) where entrance is gained to a cave which contains many evidences that the cave was occupied as living quarters by a large group of humans for many years. The cave is supposed to contain gold bars, Spanish treasure chests, church treasures, jeweled crowns, precious stones and the workings from which the gold was extracted and cast into bars. The value of the treasure is claimed to exceed $22,000,000."

The report states Noss revealed to Herkenhoff the names of several persons claiming an interest in the treasure, listing, among others:

Mr. Holt of Lordsburg, N.M.
Mr. Robinson, Los Angeles
Mr. Mullins, New Mexico Educational Association
Mr. Barber, Albuquerque
Mr. Ponder, Albuquerque
Mr. Weddon, Sonora, Texas
Mr. Johnson, Hatch, N.M.
Mr. Wagoner, Socorro

"The whole truth"

The files at the Land Office contain numerous affidavits, most signed and notarized, that support Noss' treasure claims. In one such document a B. D. Lampros is described as visiting Noss at his encampment at the peak and being handed a chunk of gold ore. Lampros, the affidavit relates, took the ore to an assay firm, Holly & Holly, in Douglas, Arizona, and "it was found that this roughly volcanic formation ran over $5,000 in gold per ton."

Another notarized affidavit, bearing the signature of Ted Farnsworth, dated December 2, 1952, recounts that Farnsworth was at the peak in 1941, was given a sawed-off piece of gold, and took it to Los Angeles where "an assay at Zimmerman's laboratory" revealed "it ran very high, about 900 fine".

The statement then adds: "In my opinion Doc Noss was at times almost or very near a nervous breakdown, not knowing what to do with the vast fortune for fear of losing it or his life . . ."

Another statement discloses that C. D. Patterson, identified as the mayor of Portales, New Mexico, appeared before a notary in 1952 to give, in his words, "the whole truth":

"I believe I know Doc M. E. Noss as well as any person living today. I have had several heart-to-heart talks with him and I felt he spoke the truth as to his find in Victoria Peak. He offered to show me what he had taken out before it caved in, and said he had taken out almost one hundred. He went over to a bush and pulled out a bar from underneath. I was amazed at what I saw. This one was sawed in two, and looked like gold all the way through; beautiful yellow, golden. It was longer than it was wide, and was about three inches thick, and weighed around twenty pounds, about forty pounds before it was cut in half. Knowing how people go wild and crazy when they see gold, we never talked about our conversation when we returned to the house ... That man went through many trials and tribulations and then was killed before he ever got to finish opening the cave he said he found, and which I am sure he found."

The name of an E. F. Foreman also appears in the files in the following affidavit:

"I visited Hembrillo basin in July, 1944, and found Doc and his helpers at work trying to remove dirt which had closed the entrance to the cave ... I had the opportunity to see some of the relics and some of the bars of gold which Doc said he had taken from the cave ... I saw one large bar which weighed about 40 lbs. ... "

An affidavit bearing the name of Don Breech, of Portales, reveals that "Doc needed a truck of some kind to haul supplies out to the camp, so I loaned him one of mine. While I was visiting (at the peak) Doc showed me several bars which looked like gold. Some of these had holes drilled in them, and showed the same contents as deep as the drill hole went. In my estimation, Doc had found just what he said he had."

In other notarized statements there were similar attestations:

Leo D. O'Connell: "In 1942, Noss told me of his find so I decided to quit my work and help him open it. I immediately went to the basin and started work and he showed me gold bricks out of the mine, and his enthusiasm and what he showed me was evidence enough to convince me. I saw four gold bricks and tested them with acid which convinced me that it was gold and not copper."

O'Connell, a heavy equipment operator at Duchesne, Utah, told reporter Howard Bryan of the Albuquerque Tribune in mid-1973 that Noss had buried 53 bars of gold near Victoria Peak and that he moved this gold to another hiding place the night before he was killed.

Eppie Montoya, Santa Fe, in the presence of a notary: "In May, 1941, I went to work for Doc Noss at Hembrillo basin to excavate for a treasure which Noss said he had found. During my stay I saw some bars . . . which he had taken out of Victoria Peak. One brick which I held and examined was larger at the bottom than at top, slanting up on all sides, and weighing approximately twenty to twenty-five pounds. Doc told me that there were a great many more in the cave that had caved in. Dirt and rubbish had to be removed to get to the room. At the time that I saw this bar there were four or five people present."

Noss became acquainted with a Carl W. Horzman, an attorney of Lordburg, N.M., in the early 1940's. He confided details of his discovery and persuaded Horzman to agree to represent him in the event there were problems with the government.

Recalling the occasion, Horzman said he was "rather skeptical" about the treasure story, "until Noss showed me a bar of gold." At one point, Horzman related, Noss came to his office "rather upset; he said he was ready to lift the main treasure but was afraid of the government. He had deposited several bars of gold with the U. S. Mint in Denver and had got a receipt for over $97,000 but no money. The mint told him he would get paid as soon as he turned over the rest of the gold. He said he had the receipt with him but I did not ask to see it. I did not see him again."

It is a speculation as to whether these attestations to the genuineness of Noss' claims would be admissible in court upon trial of the issue of ownership. In some instances a preliminary qualifying of the documents might be difficult, the passage of time being so great. Still, the stories of some witnesses to the Noss discovery are defensible. At least two young men, it now appears certain, were at the scene when Doc Noss was removing gold from the caverns prior to 1949 — Joe Andregg who worked for Noss at the peak, and Benny Samaniego of Las Cruces.

Years later Samaniego was interviewed by Chester R. Johnson, then an associate in the Museum of New Mexico research division. In the course of that conversation Samaniego revealed that he worked for Noss at the peak and on one occasion "followed Doc Noss to see where he got his gold".

Samaniego said he was in one of the treasure rooms on the day an argument took place between Noss and the dynamiter, Montgomery, as to the best place to set off the charge. In that brief stay in the treasure room he saw "several stacks of gold bars, skeletons, armor, old guns and statues". Before he left he scratched his name on one of the bars.

Unlike Samaniego, Andregg did not enter the treasure rooms. In fact, Noss permitted no outsider even to approach the shaft entrance. Andregg said he did not go beyond the first ledge, a mere 50 feet below the surface.

Noss had yet another young helper in the early months following his discovery, Jose Serafin Sedillo, who lived in nearby Rincon. Sedillo was put to work securing ropes and ladders and generally assisting with preparations for descents into the treasure rooms.

Though accounts differ as to who, besides Noss, actually entered the rooms, Jose seems to have made one trip only. On that occasion he carried two gold bars to the surface, which Noss quickly seized. He told Noss they were his and he wanted them back. Noss quickly and effectively divested the youth of such a wild notion by brandishing a rifle. Incensed, Jose left the area. Several years later, following Noss' death, he returned with his wife, Ella, at the request of Mrs. Noss, mostly to keep watch at the site. The couple lived in the stone house for a considerable period, probing crevices near the collapsed shaft. They found nothing, eventually packed their belongings and left the basin permanently.

It is not easy to justify or explain the numerous arrangements between Noss and outsiders without conceding the existence of a treasure. Individuals with temperament and habit entirely alien to adventuring took more than a passing interest in his predicament. Informally, money would be given on a mere verbal assurance that the donor would be generously remembered when Noss got his hands on the treasure.

Now and then a handful of investors would contribute a modest per-capita share, often recording the informal understandings in a crudely prepared memo. Noss himself rarely signed such documents.

In the 5-year period following the collapse of the shaft there were several collective efforts of this sort, mainly to help defray costs in Noss' attempts to re-open the passage.

One such enterprise, in 1941, was structured by a person ostensibly with some legal background. Proper documents were prepared and signed, and an engineer was consulted. What exactly was accomplished by the syndicate is not apparent in the records, though it was under one such arrangement that a fairly passable road was built along the thirty miles from Rincon (nearest town to Victoria Peak) to the rim of Hembrillo basin, replacing a primitive wagon trail that resisted passage with the vagaries of wind, rain and erosion.

As could be foreseen, the number of would-be partners and benefactors increased materially after the cave-in, concurrent with Noss' peddling of a gold bar here and there, and when the rumor mills were at their busiest.

Offers of genuine interest were not easily segregated from proposals concealing sharp tactics. But to the outsider, Noss' own position was something less than edifying: He was seeking donations of money while ostensibly in possession of a vast treasure, a kind of poverty-stricken Croesus.

Little wonder negotiations were apt to end suddenly and inexplicably. Agreements easily made were quickly breached. Noss was able to view these sudden twists and turns somewhat stoically. Bare-handed instances of profligacy or betrayal were not so easily absorbed; often he took to drinking out of frustration or anger.

The story is told that one day, detecting a plot designed to relieve him of some gold by trickery, Noss appeared at the home of the would-be cheat, pretending to be drunk. He waved a package shaped like a brick, then offered to sell the package sight unseen for two hundred dollars. Seeing him weaving and prancing drunkenly about the room, the conspirator concluded that here was an opportunity to make a killing. He handed over the money, received the package and before he could ascertain that he had bought a gold-painted brick Noss was off and away into the night.

The early days

Ova was born in 1895 in Saffordville, Kansas, not far from Great Bend. A sturdy woman of extraordinary energy she was, in the words of a friend, "tough as a steer's horn and durable as a cactus." Her maiden name was Coltrup. She was the second youngest in a family of seven children, five boys and two girls — Will, Charlie, Orlie, Cecil, Amy, Ova and Irl. The father, John Coltrup, a lawyer, was appointed to a state judgeship and rode the Oklahoma circuit for many years.

The family homesteaded in Oklahoma at the turn of the century, lived for a spell in a small town not far from Enid. Ova spoke with pride of the fact the children, except Amy, Irl and herself, became school teachers, each having acquired the then all-important state life certificate.

In 1918, at 23, Ova married Roy Beckwith, a railroad freighthouse worker. "I met him while I was playing the piano for dances in Oklahoma. I played for dances all over the country. I also taught music. I traveled with the Chautauqua for over two years. What kind of music did I play? Mostly ballroom music. I met Roy at a dance. I was playing and he just sashayed around me. He kept calling and finally I married him. We had four children, Letha, Dorothy, Marvin and Harold. We lived most of the time in Tonkawa, Oklahoma, close to Ponca. Roy and I were married twelve years and we got a divorce in 1929."

After the divorce, Ova moved to Oklahoma City. There she met a self-proclaimed foot doctor named Milton

Ernest (Doc) Noss. "He fixed up my infected toe and asked me if I wanted to go fishing, and I did and we kept going together. One day he just up and demanded that I marry him. We had a wonderful life. He treated me good."

Doc was not without some local repute, though his practice rarely involved anything more complicated than an ankle sprain or a throbbing toenail. He was also sought after for advice on mining matters, mostly by landed proprietors holding valuable mining permits.

Ova rejected the local gossip that Doc went on frequent drunken sprees: "Here was the trouble. After he found the treasure, he would try to do something and then if he failed at it, like when he went to the Denver mint and didn't get his money, he would stay on a drunk for days, just damn mad at the world."

She said Indians and whites "married down there in Oklahoma then. Doc was Cheyenne on his mother's side. His father was German and spelled his name K-n-a-u-s, not N-o-s-s."

Doc and Ova were married in Sayre, Oklahoma, a union that lasted more than twelve years. In late November, 1945, Noss was granted a decree of divorce by the chancery court of Pulaski County, Arkansas, Cause No. 74511 — an action that was to precipitate a long controversy over the separate claims of the first Mrs. Noss and the second Mrs. Noss.

Noss next courted Violet Lena Boles, married her in Pulaski county on August 8, 1947. Shortly after Noss' death in 1949 Violet married Roy B. Yancy.

When the treasure trove gained national attention in 1969 she filed an affidavit in Tarrant County, Texas, stating that no child or children was ever born to Milton E. Noss, no child or children was ever adopted by him, that Doc had died without a will, that she inherited all of the property as his wife at the time of his death, including the mining claims in New Mexico and "any hidden treasure, mines or mineral on state lands." She claimed ownership in 76 percent of the Victoria Peak treasures.

One day I asked Ova about Noss' divorce action.

"The story came out that Doc had got the divorce for desertion," she said. "But I was never served with a notice of the divorce. He got it somewhere in Arkansas. I never did desert him. I was teaching music and playing the piano at the Silver Slipper night club and holding down all kinds of jobs. He was supposed to have got the divorce in 1945 or 1946, early January, I think, but he came back to see me and stayed around, and one time he stayed almost a week. That was just before the shooting. I was working in Hot Springs and Doc was looking for ways to make money so we would get some equipment back on Victoria Peak. He decided to go to Alice, Texas, and work in the oil fields there for a spell and that is how he met the man who shot and killed him. They said it was self-defense. That's what the jury said."

It must not be imagined that Noss' behavior was motivated entirely by his dilemma over the treasure. Being part white caused him to struggle against the forces that antagonized him. Torn by desire for recognition or at least acceptance he behaved rudely to appease his pride and express his contempt for society. Often, fortified with liquor, he tested the patience of law enforcement officers in Las Cruces, Hot Springs or Hatch with blustering barroom exhibitions, sometimes waving a pistol. The reaction of the constabulary to these outbursts was tempered with more compassion than the occasions seemed to warrant. They understood him; a roistering half-breed with one too many under his belt. In most instances they escorted him to jail for an overnight return to sobriety.

All in all, the police entries on Noss comprise mostly odds and ends — numerous arrests for drunken and disorderly behavior, two or three minor convictions or fines. In 1935, the most serious of the charges — "Insulting while armed" — landed him in a state prison for four months.

After the divorce, which she was convinced was not valid, Ova Noss made it plain she did not have the slightest intention of withdrawing or surrendering her interest in the treasure trove. Noss had failed to give her proper notice of the court action and, further, there was no agreement of any kind as to the division of the couple's property. She was now more determined than ever to claim a good share, if not all, of the treasure trove. She considered it her due. After all, it was Ova Noss who appeared at the Land Office in Santa Fe year after year, applied for and received the annual permit to continue mining activities at Victoria Peak. She signed every application and, as far as the Land Office knew, she alone had the authority to prospect on New Mexican land. From her point of view, Doc had abandoned the project.

Even with the collapse of the shaft she kept working at Victoria Peak, using a crude, largely ineffective lifting mechanism to remove small scoops of debris from the shaft. Occasionally she was helped by her sons, Marvin mostly, and daughters, along with a close friend or two.

Doc, meanwhile, aware how costly it would be to bring in equipment and men for a professional job, took to searching for another entry to the mine, one that would not require extensive excavating work. The search took him a considerable distance from the old opening and it was that activity that caused Ova to speculate on the possibility her ex-husband was prospecting in another area — without a permit! She would prefer to conclude that what remained in the treasure caverns was hers, Doc having thoughtlessly waived his right to claim entitlement to any of it. Valid or not, her reasoning was academic at the time — for the gold was deep in bowels of the earth, far beyond human reach.

It was the State Land Office's policy to maintain a continuity as to permits issued to prospectors, farmers or cattlemen. It was first come, first served. A permit must be obtained each year. A permit granted for one year did not necessarily entitle the applicant to a permit for the same project the following year. But the Land Office always favored the punctual applicant. If an application was granted for one year, the same would be granted the following year — unless the applicant failed to apply in timely fashion or had violated the terms of the permit in the previous year.

At all times the Land Office assured Ova Noss — once by letter from the then Land Office commissioner — that she would be given priority over any other person, as long as she made timely application for an annual permit.

In the late winter of 1946, less than a year after Noss' divorce, Ova applied to the State for a permit that would allow her to conduct mining operations on Victoria Peak. The permit, if granted, would give her the right to conduct much broader activities at the Peak than had been given her in previous permits. She had another reason for asking; she wanted to take whatever step was necessary to keep her ex-husband off the hill. A grant of a mining permit would foreclose another major avenue to him.

At this time Land Office officials were preparing to authorize a routine inspection of operations in the area, including those atop Victoria Peak, largely to determine whether holders of permits were working their claims diligently and observing the ground rules. But there was more basis for the inspection this time, notably the much greater public interest in the goings-on at the Peak. The Land Office decided on a more scientific inspection and hired a field engineer named Donn Clippinger in the fall of 1948 to determine whether a gold vein could exist in the Victoria Peak area. In this way the Land Office could put to rest the rumors that gold could have been mined and shaped into bars within caverns at the peak. It didn't turn out quite that way.

Clippinger reached the location (Section 16, T 16 S., R. 3 E., Socorro-Dona Ana counties) by traveling northeast approximately 33 miles from Rincon on a graded road formerly used by a talc company, trucking its product from the San Andres mountains to the railroad at Rincon. Nearing the basin he found his progress impeded here and there by small block-faulted hills. Victoria Peak, a 400-foot conical hill rising abruptly from the canyon floor, did appear to Clippinger to bear interesting formations — Paleozoic limestone, thin beds of Pennsylvanian shales, strata of dense dark green sandstone.

In his formal report Clippinger noted "the existence of an orebody exposed in Victoria Peak by the caverns . . . is not only possible but highly probably . . . Samples taken (from Victoria Peak) assayed a trace of gold. These proposed claims are certainly worthy of further investigation."

After the Clippinger report, the Land Office granted Ova a mineral permit, advised her that annual application would keep her name at the top of the list for that specific area.

Then came the big surprise: In a special letter to permit-holders, state officials revealed that negotiations were going on between the state of New Mexico and the Department of Defense. The object: Condemnation of thousands of acres to be used by the U. S. Army for the testing of missiles produced at Los Alamos. The far-reaching lease arrangement of 25 years' duration would involve nearly 5,000 acres.

The formal signing was certain; prospecting time now was limited. Quickly, notices were in the mail advising one and all that renewal of future permits was most unlikely.

Because of different expirations, some prospectors

were served notices and soon left their diggings, permanently. Farms were dismantled. Range people sold or relocated their stock.

The state's agreement with the military restricted use only to the *surface* of the land. New Mexico retained the mineral and mining rights relating to below-the-surface operations.

The Noss family, however, was not among the departing ones; Victoria Peak had not yet been included in the condemned acreage.

Surmising the government's encroachment would not reach the peak, Noss and Ova spent many a summer night at the desert camp, occasionally with one or more of Ova's youngsters. They took turns at the shaft, attacking debris which they knew separated them from wealth and a life of comfort. The family recalled nights spent on canvas cots, often curled around a bar of gold. They remembered how Doc would retrieve the bars the next morning and hide them at some place out of their sight. One of the daughters remembered she had a bar under her bed at home for a considerable period, until reclaimed by the ever-cautious stepfather. Before the shaft was sealed off, their most vivid memory was of the excitement and curiosity generated by Noss upon his return from the caves carrying a canvas bag. True to form, he would take the treasure to some distant hiding place.

The shooting

Charles Ryan was a tall, lean, striking figure with an easy, amiable manner, the more handsome for a shock of white hair. In his home town of Alice, Texas, folks esteemed Charley. He owned a shop that specialized in the repair of oil field equipment, endearing himself to local residents by a neighborly willingness to help them through mechanical crises.

Ryan had heard about the treasure trove legend from various sources, mostly newspaper stories. He was intrigued. One day in the winter of '48, Ryan showed up in Hatch, not so much looking for Doc Noss, though that was also on his mind, but primarily to find out whether there was anything at all to the gold story.

The two met and got along superbly well. Noss found Ryan to be an agreeable person, candid and friendly. Ryan wanted to know about the gold and Noss was eager to oblige. He detailed his find at Victoria Peak and assured Ryan there would be a number of gold bars for sale. And at a good price, too.

Noss spent some time in Alice and there was more conversation about the treasure. Ultimately a deal was made: Noss would sell Ryan "a few gold bars" for $25,000. Ryan would come to Hembrillo basin by private plane landing on a makeshift runway just over the saddle. There the exchange would take place — gold for cash. On the day agreed upon the plane came down, Ryan emerged and asked Noss to hand over the gold bars.

Noss said the bars were hidden nearby. But first he wanted the $25,000. Ryan said he would produce the money when Noss handed over the gold.

The two argued at some length, then proceeded to nearby Hatch to a house which the Ryans had rented.

A few minutes later Noss was observed hastily leaving the house, visibly agitated, running toward his truck, parked a short distance away.

Ryan appeared on the porch, a gun in hand. A voice was heard, probably emanating from the house, shouting: "Shoot the dirty son-of-a-bitch!"

Ryan shot and missed.

The voice: "Shoot again!"

The second bullet struck Noss in the head. He died instantly as he fell near the truck, an arm partly draped over the front bumper.

Upon arraignment, Ryan entered a plea of self-defense.

. Noss (straddling pole) atop Victoria
k in the months she and helpers
ght to excavate the collapsed shaft.

This crude "windlass" was used by Mrs. Noss in her efforts to remove debris from the collapsed shaft. Photo taken 8/3/51.

The trial

The case of the State of New Mexico vs. Charley Ryan was heard on May 25 and 26, 1949, before a jury in the third judicial district courtroom of Judge W. T. Scroggin, Dona Ana County.

Seven witnesses were presented by the state, five of them mine workers who were at the scene of the murder and saw the shooting.

The defense would produce thirty-two witnesses, principally to testify as to their knowledge of Doc Noss' reputation.

The state's first witness was Willard L. Blake, an unemployed truck driver. He said he was working for Ryan and Noss at some mining claims not far from Victoria Peak and on the day of the shooting, Saturday, March 5, he had gone to Ryan's house in Hatch with four other workmen, riding in Ryan's jeep. He and four fellow workers went to the house to be paid for their week's work.

The witness said he left the jeep and walked toward the house to turn over the time sheet to Buck Harris, an associate of Ryan. Ryan and Doc came out as he approached.

"He pulled his gun," Blake said.

"Who pulled his gun?"

"Charley Ryan."

"What did he do with it?"

"Pulled the hammer back and pointed it at Doc Noss and told him to get back into the house. I stepped back and Ryan marched him back into the house."

"Explain how he marched him into the house."

"He pointed the gun toward his back."

Blake said he could hear them "arguing and talking very loud," but could not determine what they were saying.

Blake said he returned to the jeep. "I told the boys about Ryan pulling the gun . . . . . and I had not been there but a few minutes when I saw the dining room window break (Doc Noss had pushed Ryan against it in an outburst of anger), then I saw Doc Noss come running out of the house. Ryan came running out behind him. Ryan shot at him. Ryan hollered, "Come out from under there you son-of-a-bitch," and someone else yelled from the house, 'Shoot that son-of-a-bitch' and Ryan shot the second time.

The witness said he and his four companions "took out," running west, "because we were afraid."

He said they stopped at a residence down the street and asked a young man to call the sheriff's office.

Shortly, two deputies arrived at the house and took Ryan to the jail at Hatch.

Asked whether he saw anything unusual in Ryan's appearance at the time of the killing, Blake replied,

"He was kind of mad looking, wild looking . . . . I never did see him look like that."

Under questioning by a defense attorney the witness said he had seen Noss carry a gun at the mine site. "When it wasn't in his holster he kept it in the glove compartment."

"In the glove compartment of the pickup truck that was parked in front of Ryan's house (on the day of the shooting)?"

"Yes."

The witness said that after the second shot he saw Noss fall in front of the truck on the left side of the truck — at the driver's, not the glove compartment side.

Except for minor differences, the testimony of Ollan Ray Brown, the state's second witness, was the same as Blake's.

Asked if he heard Noss shout, "I will kill all you sons-a-bitches," Brown replied he had not.

His testimony corroborated Blake's version of where Noss fell after the second bullet penetrated his brain — "half on the front bumper with his head on his arm and his feet stretched out."

The defense asked Brown why Noss, Ryan and others wore guns at the mines.

"The only thing I heard - I didn't hear Noss say it — I heard some of the men talking about it, said he might have trouble with his ex-wife, Ova Noss.

"Did you ever see where Mrs. Noss was then working with her crew?"

"No, sir."

"Did you learn that they were working about a mile from you folks?"

"I learned they were working on some mountain out there."

"You were out there on Friday. On the day before this happened, was there a plane crash?"

"Yes."

"Did you learn that one of Doc's first wife's boys was in the plane?"

"I knew it was some kin."

"Were you there when those boys were brought into the doctor's?"

"I was out on the job."

"Did you go over to where the plane crashed?"

"Yes."

"Did you help load them in the pickup to take them to the doctor?"

"No, sir."

Next, Pedro Nunoz testified he was employed by Ryan

for pick-and-shovel work at the mines. In his version of the shooting, he placed Noss at a point equally distant between the house and the pickup when Ryan, standing on the house steps, fired the first shot.

At that point the witness said he heard someone shout, "Shoot the son-of-a-bitch again," but he asserted he did not hear Ryan say anything.

Two other witnesses, brothers, William Brizendine and Denver Brizendine, testified that as Doc came out of the house and started toward the truck, Ryan told him to stop. "Doc didn't and he fired one shot. Doc kept going and he fired another shot."

The first person to enter the Ryan residence after the shooting was Paul Maubry, a deputy sheriff. He testified he found Ryan in the kitchen and Harris in the hallway.

"Mrs. Ryan was in the bedroom crying. I asked Ryan who did the shooting. He said he did. I asked him where the gun was. He said it was lying on the kitchen cabinet."

Deputy Sheriff Roy Sandman, last of the state's witnesses, testified he removed a .38-caliber pistol and a cartridge belt with eighteen bullets from the glove compartment of Noss' pickup truck shortly after he and Maubry arrived at the scene.

Except for minor differences the testimony of the other state witnesses was essentially the same as the others at the scene.

Toward evening of the first day of the trial, about 7:30, the defense began its case.

The defense elected to make a brief opening statement, the central premise of which was that Ryan shot Noss under circumstances in which Ryan had full reason to fear for his life, in brief:

"Noss went to work for Mr. Ryan at his tool company in Alice, Texas, about four and a half months previous to the time this trouble arose at Hatch .... Noss would visit with Mr. and Mrs. Ryan and began telling them about mining claims he had out here in New Mexico. He told them he had valuable lead and silver claims and he felt he should get back here and take care of them. He said he had been away some time and the mines had been neglected. Mr. Ryan was in bed with a sprained ankle at the time and Noss finally induced Mr. Ryan to come out here. Ryan drove his car to Santa Fe. He offered to give Doc Noss $1,000 and also offered to let Noss use his truck to go to Las Cruces and tend to the mines. Doc Noss insisted Ryan come with him and finally prevailed upon him to do it. They came out and later filed on some fifteen supposedly valuable lead claims. Some were supposed to bear silver and others, according to Noss, also had uranium in them. From the time he came up here, in fact, before he left Alice, Texas, Noss said 'These people up here are dangerous, this is very valuable property I have and we have to be armed.' He induced Mr. Ryan to purchase this gun for himself, the one which has the wooden handle, and another one for Noss .... The mining claims were proven worthless from a commercial standpoint. We have some assays showing that they bore some four percent lead instead of eighty, and no uranium whatever. We also expect to show that Doc Noss bore a reputation in each community he visited in the State of New Mexico that we are cognizant of, of being quarrelsome and dangerous."

The state attorney objected: We do want to point out that much of what the defense is saying will prove to be inadmissible evidence. Objection.

The Court: Overruled.

The defense attorney continued: We are going to show specific acts of violence on the part of Doc Noss in every community he was in — Alamogordo, Socorro, out at the mines — that he was habitually a gun-toter, that he threatened people's lives on a number of occasions and we have the witnesses here. Those things will be brought before you. We have a number of witnesses on all these various items of general reputation.

State: Your Honor, that is argument as to how many witnesses they have.

The Court: I think so, too.

Defense: We expect to prove by oral testimony of witnesses that his reputation for truth and veracity was bad, that he was a gun-toter, that he was quarrelsome and dangerous. Getting down to the shooting on the 5th day of March, we expect to show you that Mr. Ryan had been away from his business some time and decided he would go back to Alice, Texas. He sent Jack Lawrence and Doc Noss out to bring the men in so they could be paid. He was going to Texas. They went out and came back and the boys working for Mr. Ryan were asked to come there for their pay. Noss came in the house where the Ryans and Jack Lawrence were living at Hatch. On that occasion he informed Mr. Ryan he was not going back to Texas and the truck was not going back to Texas. He said he wanted Mr. Ryan to loan him $350, that he had some gold he wanted to take to El Paso and have it rerun so he could take it to Arizona and dispose of it. Mr. Ryan said, "I am not going to let you use my truck for that purpose, I am not going to give you $350 or any other amount." He went out to ask Blake about the jeep and he found out they had both been to the filling station at eleven o'clock. Doc Noss told him they had been there at eleven o'clock. It was the first time it had been missing and due to the fact that it had not been returned, Mr. Ryan and Mr. Lawrence made a ninety-mile trip looking for the boys, feeling that something had happened to them, but they later found out that Doc had told them to take the jeep. Doc came out and Mr. Ryan had his pistol in his pocket. He said, "Doc go back in the house and we will discuss this matter." Blake finally got the time in there and Mr. Ryan went back in the house and Doc said, "If you don't let me have this $350 I will kill you — it means $220,000 to me." Mr. Ryan said, "I don't care. I don't want to have anything to do with an

47

illegitimate deal of that kind." When Mr. Ryan came back in the house he handed his gun to Mr. Lawrence. Then he went in and took his position by the window. When he told him he wouldn't let him have it, Doc Noss hit him and ran out and said, "I will kill every one of you sons-of-bitches." Mr. Ryan grabbed the gun from Mr. Lawrence and went out and fired one shot to try to stop him and then another one which resulted fatally.

Ryan took the witness stand near the start of the second day of trial. He gave his age as 39. He said he had been in oil-field repair work and machine-shop welding "about twenty-five years, all my life."

Asked to give a brief history of his connections with Noss from the time he met him and all his dealings with him up to the time he came out to New Mexico, he testified:

"Noss applied for a job in November, 1948, during my absence and Mr. Shell, my bookkeeper, hired him. He was there a couple or three days before I came back. I told him he couldn't work with the truck he had. He asked me to loan him the money to buy a truck. I told him I couldn't do that. After talking to him awhile I decided that I would buy him a truck and told him he could pay me back at $100 a month. In the meantime he had told me about having this money owing to him, so we went by the Bishop bank at Bishop, Texas. Mr. Buck, president of the bank, verified the statement of Noss that a Mr. Smith owed him $760 and had agreed to mail a check into the bank to deposit in Noss' account. After we left the bank we went to look at some trucks. The officers drove up and asked who was driving this Dodge truck."

State: We object, your Honor. This is getting into the realm of hearsay.

Defense: Hearsay as to who?

State: He is quoting a statement he heard, hearsay statement.

Defense: As I understand it, the defendant is entitled to lay his story before the jury.

The Court: I think I will let him go ahead.

Ryan: The officers drove up and asked who was driving this Dodge truck. The car salesman pointed to Noss. They walked over and told him he was under arrest. I was in my car, I got out and walked over and asked the officer what the trouble was. He said he was under arrest for giving worthless checks.

State: Objection, your Honor. This is all hearsay.

The Court: Overruled.

Defense: We are willing to let their objection go to all this line to save objecting all the time. I think the witness is entitled to the right of being permitted to narrate this story.

The Court: Proceed, Mr. Ryan.

Ryan: I went down to the jail to see what the fine would be. Noss asked me to come down. I happened to talk to Mr. Martin, County Attorney at Corpus Christi. He said he had some checks there. He showed me some checks. He said, "Do you want to make $2,500?" I said, "No." He said, "As soon as he hits the street I will arrest him on the other. I am going to send him to the penitentiary." I told him I thought he was trying to send an innocent man to the penitentiary. They brought Noss down from the jail and he told Martin the checks would not exceed $85. I gave Mr. Martin my check for $150.

Q. At that time was there any talk to the bank over the telephone?

A. Yes, Mr. Martin called Mr. Buck over at Bishop at the bank. So he asked me would I take care of any additional checks that were out. I told him no, because I didn't know how many checks would be out. After Noss came down he turned him over to me. It wasn't but a few days after that until I got a letter from Martin.

Q. You left how much money with him?

A. $150 the first time. I got the letter from Mr. Martin

that the $150 was used up and he had some more checks that were returned. At that time I believe it was $37. I sent my check for the difference. That happened three times before I got the checks paid off Noss had written. The same day he was in jail, when we came back home, there was a long distance phone call, he had given a man two $50 checks in McAllen. The man was going to turn them over for collection. Mr. Martin had told him the next time a check came in he was going to send him to the penitentiary, I couldn't pay it all; I hated to see this man in trouble, so I told this man to run them on through. I called Mr. Buck at the Bishop bank and told him to okay the $100 worth of checks and I would mail him my check, which I did. Noss said that was all the checks he had out. The day we left Alice to come to New Mexico he came to me with a note on the Bishop bank for $289, asked me if I would sign it. I said, "What is this?" He said, "Some checks Mr. Buck has been holding." I signed that note for him. It is at the Bishop bank now.

Q. That note was never paid?

A. Never paid for Noss. No, sir, none of them were.

Q. What now led up to your coming to New Mexico with Noss?

A. After we got back to the shop and I had paid this last $100 worth of checks for him I told him he couldn't work for me and give hot checks or get drunk and not pay his bills because I didn't tolerate that. He in turn began complimenting my business and said how well people spoke of me. I said, "Yes, it's like owning a gold mine if you can't sell the gold." That's the way the gold and the lead claims came in. He started talking to me about this treasure. One night about 11 o'clock he got a phone call from Mr. Parr in Freona, Texas, telling him that his former wife was trying to obtain a permit on this mountain where this treasure is supposed to be. Noss said he just had to go to Santa Fe. I was in bed with a sprained ankle. I told him to go ahead, but no, he wanted me to go. After a long talk I got up out of bed and we left. He drove my car to Santa Fe. After we got to Santa Fe we learned that the state had already given Mrs. Noss a permit. We stayed around a couple days, talked to the Attorney General and the Assistant Attorney General. I told them that the only reason I was there was that I felt sorry for the man. Noss told me people up here had stole from him, tried to kill him, that I was the only honest man he had ever found. I told the Attorney General I was there to help Mr. Noss, I didn't want to get connected with it. I had a business which required all my time. After we got back home Noss finds out he couldn't get this permit on this (treasure) cave. He started talking about lead claims, silver claims that were worth lots of money. He had a cross rock up here which he said he had to get out of New Mexico. There was four of us came out here, stayed about four weeks during the bad weather to try to get this cross rock.

"What do you mean by cross rock?"

"A rock about so long with a square cut on it. I never could figure out how it entered the picture, but he claimed it was very valuable. While we was here we checked the records, and we claimed a mining permit on the lead and silver claims. Me being inexperienced in the mining business, all I could go by was what he told me. He got me interested and after I got back home I told him I would loan him $1,000 and let him bring the pickup here. I said, 'I don't want to fool with it, when you get through with it you can pay me back.' He said no, he couldn't operate unless I was up here. Mr. Lawrence and Mr. Harris were pretty good friends of mine. I talked to those boys and asked them if they would go in on this thing I would put some money in it and they could stay here to operate it. I came out here to stay about a week to see what kind of equipment they needed, and I was going back to my business. Everytime anything was said about going back they said they couldn't do anything without me, I had to stay. Noss told me the lead would run from 50 to 80 percent lead. I looked at him, I didn't know anything about it. The ore had plenty of weight to it. After we were here a couple of weeks working on it I had found out you could take this ore and have an assay run on it and find out what it was. We had three assays run and it showed 6.8 percent lead.

"Who did the assay work?"

"Cricket and Ferguson."

"I show you an envelope with two assay returns, is that this run?"

"Yes."

"Have you ever seen these assays before?"

"No, these are the last ones we had run. After we got the first assay back and it showed only 6 to 8 percent lead Noss said, 'When you get down a little deeper it will be a whole lot better.' We hired some men to clean out the shaft and we had the second assay run, it came back the same way. I didn't think too much of that. The last week we was up here during that time I had caught him in quite a few things he told me that wasn't so. The last week my wife, unfortunately, got sick so I wouldn't go out on the job."

"That was after you were at Hatch?"

"Yes, my wife was sick. We were strangers there and didn't have anyone to look after her. Noss would tell me to watch the people in New Mexico, not to talk to them. He said they would kill me when they find out I was the man putting up the money to operate this. I told him I couldn't see why anybody would want to kill me. I hadn't done anything to these people. They had no reason to feel hard toward me. Those claims were open. Anybody could make claim on them. After I got a chance to talk to a few nice people here I began to find out what kind of a man he was. I told my wife I was a little disappointed. I was disappointed in the man, I had found out he wasn't the right kind of man to do business with. The next day

I didn't go to the mine. I made it my business to talk to a few people and get some more information. On Wednesday he came to me, said he wanted to go to Douglas. He said he knew someone there that would put in a $50,000 mill to take care of the ore. I told Jack Lawrence to go with him and stay with him and listen to all the conversation. I told Jack I had found out about the man and was a little leery about him. They go to Douglas and Noss talked to the men there."

"Prior to leaving your home to come up there had you ever owned a pistol?"

"No, that is the first and only pistol I ever owned in my life."

"How did you happen to buy it?"

"Noss said it wasn't safe for he or I, or anybody, to come up here and start operating those mines without being well protected."

"At his suggestion what did you obtain?"

"I bought this pistol from the Alice Hardware in Alice, Texas. I bought it the day I left Alice to come to Hatch the last time."

"When you first came up here, how many claims, if you remember, approximately did you all locate, you and Noss and the rest of you?"

"I think altogether there were about 18 or 20 claims. One was supposed to be a lead vein about five miles long and the other was silver."

"What did you do with reference to organizing any corporation or any outfit to take care of these mining operations?"

"Well, after he told them in Santa Fe that he didn't want anything in his name, that due to the trouble he was having with his former wife in this treasure deal he would be sued, so all those claims had to be in my name. I agreed to that, but I told him we would have to form a corporation due to the fact that I had business in Texas and I didn't want to have a partnership business in New

Mexico, that it would have to be a corporation, so I told him I wanted to go to some reliable attorney to draw these corporation papers up. He recommended you. He said you had been his attorney, so that is when I first met you, when you drew up the corporation papers for me."

"You and he came to my office and you say I prepared the initial papers for you?"

"Yes, sir."

"Did that deal ever go through, did you consummate the filing of the papers?"

"No, sir, I did not."

"Along about that time did you have occasion to consult any mining engineer for the purpose of going out there to investigate these claims?"

"Yes, I met Mr. Walters at Socorro. I believe he was Dean of the Socorro School of Mines about 23 years. He gave me quite a lot of information on the mining business. I obtained a special deputy sheriff's commission in Socorro County to carry a pistol. I had never carried one before and I didn't want to be arrested for carrying a pistol without a permit. When I went into the sheriff's office in Socorro the sheriff told me I would have to have a $500 bond to carry a pistol. He asked me if I could get a bond signed. I told him I didn't know anyone. I went over to a lawyer's office and asked him if he would sign it. He said he couldn't because he was Assistant District Attorney. I asked who was Master of the Masonic Lodge. He said he didn't know, to go over to the drug store, the man there could tell me. I went over to the drug store, introduced myself to the druggist, who is a Mason, and he said he would sign it. He introduced me to Mr. Walters, and Mr. Walters signed the bond for me. After that I got pretty well acquainted with Mr. Walters and obtained quite a bit of information from him. On Thursday, prior to this accident on Saturday, I was in Socorro and I saw Mr. Walters. He said, 'How are you getting along?' I said, 'I don't believe I'm doing

54

so well.' He said, 'As soon as I file these papers I would like to talk to you.' He came out of the Court House after he filed them and we went down to his house and I talked to him for probably an hour. He didn't know prior to that that Noss was associated with me. He showed me letters from people who had written him, dated back to 1939, where Noss had swindled people in New Mexico."

State: "If the Court please, we object to that."

The Court: "I believe that is hearsay."

Defense: "Eliminate that. Don't say what the letters showed. As a result of your acquaintanceship with him state whether or not you solicited his services for the purpose of examining these mining claims you had located."

Ryan: "I told him I wanted someone to come out and make a thorough examination of these claims. We had to see whether it would be profitable to operate. Mr. Walters told me he was doing that kind of work and would be glad to check them. He asked me how much we had invested in that and I said approximately $5,000. He said for $200 he would tell us whether we have anything or not. I asked him when he could come down, he said he had to go to Santa Fe for court as a witness and he would drop me a card when he could come down. I believe when I was in jail the following week my wife got the letter from Mr. Walters telling me when he could come down. We called him and told him not to come down, that this had happened. I didn't see Mr. Walters for approximately a week after this happened."

"There was some reference yesterday by one of the boys that Doc was an engineer. Did he ever purport to you to be a mining engineer or any kind of engineer?"

"No, after we came up here he told me he had gone over to Socorro to this school and Mr. Walters had helped him considerably to where he was able to tell valuable ore when he saw it."

"While you were prospecting out there did he

demonstrate that?"

"Yes, he had a name for all those rocks and told me the claims we had were worth $87.50 a ton."

"Where, at the same time you were working the claims, if you know, was the former Mrs. Noss working?"

"She was working up on top of this mountain. We had to go by the side of it to get over to our claims."

"Had you met her and any of her associates?"

"No, I had talked to one or two of the boys when they came by there driving a bulldozer. I met Mrs. Noss, I guess, ten days prior to the 5th of March.

"About how far from your claim were they working?"

"Approximately a mile and a half."

"What, if anything, did Doc tell you about any anticipated trouble on behalf of his former wife out there at the mining claim?"

"Well, that she was about the worst woman he ever heard of, how mean she was, a bunch of thieves working over there on this cave, that you don't dare speak to them, they would kill you on sight."

"Did you go out there without guns?"

"No, Noss himself wouldn't go out there without a gun on him."

"State whether or not he was an expert shot."

"I don't know."

"What did you see him do?"

"I saw him kill a hawk sitting in a bush. He stepped it off for 63 steps."

"What else did you see him do with a pistol?"

"He killed quite a few rabbits. He would show you the rabbit's head. He would say, 'I will shoot that rabbit's head off'. If the rabbit was sitting still that is usually what happened to him."

"Is this the only gun any of you ever bought for Noss to use or carry?"

"No, we bought him, I believe, a Smith and Wesson, short barrel. That was the first gun we bought for him.

He took it home and gave it to his wife, then he carried my gun for awhile. I told him I was in El Paso in a saddle shop and saw this gun. When we went to El Paso he insisted we go by the saddle shop to look at this gun. He looked at the gun, liked it fine and told the man he would buy it.

"How did he buy it?"

"He turned around to me and told me to give the man $50, which I did."

Ryan said Doc carried the pistol in the glove compartment of his truck, which "he drove all the time."

When they met in Texas, Ryan said, he regarded Noss as "just a nice a fellow as you would want to meet. He wasn't mean.

"It was after we came to New Mexico that he got mean. When we was up in Santa Fe he and Roscoe Parr would talk about different things that they had gotten into. After we came out here he didn't ask me what to do about the business, he would do what he wanted to. He hired all these men. He didn't seem to have any respect for my position except as far as the money was concerned. As long as it didn't cost him anything."

State: If the Court please, these all seem to be conclusions.

The Court: Overruled, go ahead.

Defense: How much money did you spend at Doc Noss' suggestion out there?

State: Leading, if the Court please.

The Court: Go ahead. I don't see that it is material at this time.

"Up to that particular time, I would say $5,000 at least."

"First, in what capacity was Doc supposed to work out there, what was your arrangement on the claims?"

"He told me if I would only come up here and help him out on that that he would work for nothing. He said, 'I can take a .22 rifle and live on jack rabbits, if you will only put up the money to operate these claims.' I told him I would give him half of anything I might receive in the way of profits, as it had to be in my name. On these corporation papers you drew up I paid an attorney in El Paso $20. The attorney said to Noss, 'The only thing is I can't see how you are out of the penitentiary today.' There was five of us present."

State: That is strictly hearsay.

The Court: I don't think so. Go ahead.

Ryan: I paid the attorney $20 for the information that he wanted to find out about. After the man told him Noss had sold . . . . . .

The Court (interrupting): I think what this lawyer told him afterwards would be hearsay.

Defense: Noss was there.

The Court: Noss was there?

Defense: Yes.

The Court: Go ahead.

Ryan: He told Noss when the Government got hold of him they would send him to the penitentiary for selling these 130 shares. I told Noss when we left, I said, "You can put your name on this corporation, and that way you will know you are going to get fifty percent of the profits or whatever I may get out of it." He wouldn't do that, he never would use his name on any of the claims or the corporation papers. When we left your office he said, "I know where we can sell $50,000 worth of stock on these lead claims tomorrow." I said, "Fine." I said, "We have to have some money to operate." He said, "We won't use it to operate." He said, "I will take $25,000 and you can take $25,000." That's the first time I found out the man was crooked. I said, "Doc, not any time will I sell a man stock in a worthless corporation." I said, "The money will be deposited in the bank in my name to operate the corporation on." Therefore, he never mentioned having the corporation papers completed, and we didn't.

Ryan was asked whether Walters, the mining engineer,

visited the claims for the purpose of making an examination.

"Yes, I believe it was the 12th of April. Jack Lawrence and myself went out with him. We stayed all day looking the claims over."

"What was his report?"

"He said they wasn't worth five cents."

"Going back, will you relate any incident where Doc Noss told you of any trouble with any person at any time."

"He had told me of lots of trouble he had had with people. Of course he was innocent, all the people picked on him. The best I remember, he told me there was five people he had killed in his time. Every day when we was going to work he would say, 'There is going to be a killing today.' That went on for several days and my wife was sick and nervous and I said, 'Doc, please don't come in my house anymore saying there is going to be a killing.' He was always going to kill someone. One night he wanted to go to Hot Springs to kill Claude Fisher. I said, 'Go ahead if you want to, but you are not going to take one of my guns to kill him.' It seemed like killing people and beating people up was all he thought about."

The state attorney objected, saying the witness was drawing conclusions.

The Court replied Ryan had a right to state what his opinion is from talking to Noss.

Ryan continued: "That was his main conversation, how mean he was. I rode in with him one afternoon in the truck. He said there never was a more cold-blooded killer that ever walked the face of the earth than he was. He said you could go back to Oklahoma or New Mexico and check up on him and find out how mean he was. He said, 'I would just as soon kill you as say good morning to you.' I said, 'Why would you want to kill me? I have helped you.' He said, 'I don't mean you just now, I mean anybody if they ever do anything to me.' I said, 'Doc, I don't like to talk about those things. I have loaned you a lot of money and helped you out and I don't appreciate a man sitting around telling me he would kill me or other people'."

"Did he ever tell you about an assault he made on your stepson?"

"Yes."

State: If the Court please, that is leading in the first place. The answer would be inadmissible. I don't think specific instructions are admissible for the purpose of proving that reputation.

The Court: I think the question was leading.

The jury was excused and a conference was held before the Court, after which the objection was sustained by the Court and the defense withdrew the question.

"Mr. Ryan, coming down to the morning of the 5th of March, when you had decided to close operations, state what you did with respect to shutting down."

"On the day the plane fell out in the mountains, my truck hauled two of those boys in from there. I didn't go out. Noss had told me about his conversation with Mr. Holly in Douglas, Arizona, with respect to selling him $220,000 worth of gold Noss claimed he had hid out there somewhere. He said Mr. Holly told him, 'I almost went to the penitentiary over that last bullion I bought from you and I'm not going to buy any more unless you have it rerun.' Holly referred Noss to a man in El Paso who would rerun this bullion to where it would be one hundred percent. Jack and Noss went to El Paso and talked to this man. He wouldn't give them any satisfaction until he called Mr. Holly at Douglas, Arizona, and after the telephone conversation he agreed to rerun it for $500. Doc said, 'I got him down to $350.' That's what Noss wanted me to give him the $350 for.

"When did you close down at the mines?"

"I haven't got to that part. That was on Friday. He said he was supposed to take this gold to El Paso on Saturday night, the man was going to rerun it Saturday night and Sunday when there wasn't anybody there but himself. Noss was to pick it up Sunday night and be in Douglas on Monday. I said, 'No, Doc, I told you before I came up here that I didn't want any part of the gold because I have found out from Mr. Walters that it is against the law to have more than two ounces of gold in your possession at any time. Therefore, I don't want any part of it.'

Later, Ryan said, Noss again asked him for the $350. Ryan again refused. "I went over to the filling station. I believe I owed them about $51 for gasoline. When Jack Lawrence and Doc Noss came back from the mine they went in this station to fill up with gasoline. The boy told him he couldn't put any gas in the truck without I was there. Noss wanted to know why. He said, 'Mr. Ryan came by and told us not to charge anything else to him.' They came on to the house and we were sitting there discussing that and Noss wanted to know the reason for it. I said, 'Doc, we have spent all the money I am going to spend up here.' I have paid all the accounts and we are going back to Texas. He said, what about the $350? I told him I was not going to give him the $350.' I told him I had found out what kind of a man he is and I didn't care to be associated with him in any way, shape or form. He said he was not going back to Texas and the truck was not going back.' I said, 'Yes, the truck is going back, I don't care about you.' He said, 'You give me the $350 or I will kill you.' I said, 'You might kill me, but I am not going to give it to you.' About that time Blake and the other boys drove up in the jeep. Blake came to the door and handed me the time book. I asked Mr. Harris to figure up the time, and my wife could sign the checks. I wanted to talk to Blake. I asked Blake what time he filled up with gas Friday night. About that time Noss came out the kitchen door. I was on the step. Noss stepped off of it and said, 'God damn it, I told you what time we filled up, it was 11 o'clock.' I said, 'I didn't ask you what time you filled up." Blake never did answer me. Noss started to the truck. The gun was on the drainboard in the kitchen when I came in. I picked it up and stuck it in my pocket. I didn't want to leave it on the drainboard and go out in the yard when Noss had threatened to kill me. Noss started walking towards the truck and I said, 'Doc, don't go to the truck.' He didn't stop. I kind of jumped sideways and got between him and the truck. That is when I put my hand in my pocket and took the pistol out. I said, 'You go in the house until we get our business straightened out.' He went in the house. I never did get to talk to Blake. We walked in the house. Noss was at one end of the table. I was standing with my back to the window. Jack Lawrence was in the kitchen and I handed the gun to him as we went in. I told Noss, I said, 'I am not going to give you any money. I have had all the dealings with you I want to have. I am going to send and get the deputy sheriff and arrest you and I am going to send you to the penitentiary, you are nothing but a liar, a swindler and a thief.' When I said that Noss hit me on the chin and knocked me through the window. The only thing that kept me from going out the window was my arms. I don't know whether he hit me the second time or shoved me, but when I got on my feet I was in the far corner of the dining room and as Noss ran out the door he said, 'I will kill every one of you sons-of-bitches.' My wife was present and Jack Lawrence was present. When I started out I grabbed the gun from Lawrence and went out and fired at him once and hollered to him to stop. He made no attempt to stop. I hollered the second time to stop and as he was starting around the truck to get to the glove compartment of the truck where I knew the pistol was, I fired the second shot, and that is when he fell on the bumper."

"Why did you shoot him on that occasion?"

"He had threatened to kill me. I was afraid of him. He had already hit me in the house. He is quite a bit bigger than I am. He had bragged about how many people he had killed. I didn't want to kill him, but I was trying to protect my family, my home life, my associates."

The Court recessed for lunch, following which, direct examination of Ryan continued.

"Mr. Ryan, I believe at the noon recess you had just finished testifying as to what happened at the scene of the shooting. What did you do immediately after that?"

"I walked back in the house and told Jack Lawrence to go down and get the deputy sheriff and have him come out."

"You accompanied the officers down here to the jail in Las Cruces subsequently?"

"Yes, sir."

Ryan related Noss told him that Mrs. Noss came down to camp in a station wagon one night and shot three times at him. He finally got the gun away from her. One of her sons entered into the argument and hit Noss and knocked him loose and they all ran and got into the station wagon and drove off. Noss said he fired eight shots at the station wagon and he said it was very unfortunate he didn't kill any of them.

"The nickname 'Doc', do you know where he got it?"

"He told me he was a doctor by profession. He said over at Hot Springs he had a wonderful business and clinic until he found this hidden treasure, that he had $28,000 in the bank in Hot Springs and a good practice, and then he gave it up to keep this treasure, and that he was on the staff at the Carrie Tingley hospital as a foot specialist. I asked in Hot Springs at three drug stores if they ever knew Dr. Noss and they said no. Two of them said there used to be a woman doctor there by the name of Noss. We went out to the hospital and asked if Dr. Noss had ever been on the staff. One of these ladies there said she was there when they opened the hospital and that there definitely had never been an M. E. Noss on the staff."

Q. The day previous to this shooting what had happened with respect to any of your employees in the way of an accident?

A. That is the day this airplane fell. One of Mrs. Noss' sons was in the plane and someone else.

Q. What happened to the boys?

A. One of them got killed and one, I believe, is in the hospital in El Paso now.

Q. One is Mrs. Noss' own son?

A. Yes.

State: What is the materiality of that?

Defense: We will show it.

The Court: I don't see the materiality of it.

Defense (continued): All during the time you were operating at the mine was Mrs. Noss operating on her property?

Ryan: Yes.

Q. Were you friendly or otherwise with those people?

A. We were all friendly. The roads was bad when we first went in there. We bought a jeep and brought up their cars when they got stuck. I told my boys if any of those people got stuck to hook onto them and pull them out. I didn't have any reason for having any trouble with those people.

Q. About what age was Doc Noss?

A. Well, I don't know.

Q. His nationality?

A. He claimed to be three-fourths Indian.

Q. What tribe?

A. Cheyenne, I believe.

Q. About what was his weight at the time he worked for you?

A. I believe around 210. Very active. He was as tall as I am, maybe taller. I'm five feet 11¾ inches.

Q. This airplane accident wherein one of Mrs. Noss' sons was injured and the other boy was killed, what effect did that have on you with respect to remaining out there?

State: Your Honor, that is calling for a conclusion. We think that is objectionable.

Defense: He can state the facts.

The Court: I can't see the materiality of that airplane wreck in connection with this.

Defense (turning to the state attorney): You may cross examine.

State: "Did Noss at any time ever make any collections for you?"

"If he did he didn't turn in any money."

"You didn't trust him with the money or collections?"

"He didn't have anything to do with that."

"You say you bought a truck for him?"

"I bought the truck for him to use."

"Did you give him the title for that truck?"

"No, sir, I didn't."

"You testified as to some hot checks Doc Noss had given. How many were there altogether?"

"There was several of them, amounting to over $200."

"You paid those checks off?"

"Yes, sir."

"How long had Doc been working for you at that time?"

"At the time I paid the first checks he hadn't worked any. He was hanging around."

"How many days was it after that that you paid off these checks?"

"I believe about three days."

"Did you consider these payoffs in the form of a loss or were you making a loan?"

"I'm not in a position to be giving money away. I expected him to pay me back."

"Did you get any receipts?"

"No."

"You thought you could trust him?"

"Yes, if a man could not be trusted for that, for $200 or $300, I wouldn't want him working for me."

"You said you signed a note for him?"

"Yes. Two hundred ninety-nine and something."

"Have you paid that note off?"

"No, I went by and told Mr. Bishop about it. He said, 'Mr. Ryan, after doing what you have for that man, we will give you six months more'."

"You said you advanced him $1,000?"

"I did not. I offered to loan him $1,000 and let him take the truck and come up here. I didn't see any use in my coming up here because I didn't know anything about the mining business. I offered to loan him $1,000 and a truck because I felt sorry for him. You would have felt sorry for him. My wife even felt sorry for him."

"Then the only reason you offered him the $1,000, the only reason you paid off these checks, the only reason you offered him the right to take this truck up here is just because you felt sorry for him?"

Defense: Just a minute, he has three questions in there.

State: I will ask them separately. I will ask you if the reason you took care of those checks was because you were sorry for him?

A. Yes, because I had found out he had mining on his property. In the oil field business he had talked to Mr. Shall about that.

Q. You offered him the use of that truck just because you felt sorry for him and he had mining on his property?

A. Yes, he said he had lost this $28,000 up here and would I let him have the truck. I offered to let him bring the truck up here and give him $1,000 to give him a chance to get back on his feet.

Q. Then you had no interest in these mines in New Mexico?

A. No, sir.

Q. When you made the trip up here did you come up with the intention of taking part in the activity of opening the mine?

66

A. No, sir, I was going to put up part of the money.

Q. You made a trip to Santa Fe to get a permit?

A. To get a permit on this cave.

Q. That was supposed to have held the treasure?

A. That's right.

Q. Had he talked to you in great detail about this treasure before you left Alice?

A. Yes, he would come in my house and talk to me about it until 11 o'clock at night. After we got to Santa Fe and found out we couldn't get a permit then is when he came in and talked about the silver and lead claims that we could make millions out of. After a couple of days he came back in and said, "You remember the statement you made about this business being like a gold mine if you couldn't sell the gold?" Then he said, "I own a gold mine and can't sell the gold." That's the way the mine business started.

After a brief recess, the State continued its questioning of Ryan.

"Did the conversation about the gold take place after you paid the checks or before?"

"After I paid them."

"All the checks??"

"Not the last $289 worth, no."

"This date you talked with him the first time regarding this treasure, that was before you signed the note for him, wasn't it?"

"Yes, I didn't sign the note for him until the day we was leaving Alice to come up here."

"Mr. Ryan, you spoke of a cross rock, where was that cross rock when you first saw it?"

"They brought it to the tourist court at Hatch."

"Who?"

"Roscoe Parr, Jack Lawrence and some boy they borrowed a jeep from. He lives in Las Cruces. The road was so bad we couldn't get our cars in there. They went out in the jeep in the San Andres mountains and picked it up."

"What is it?"

"Fellow, you've got me, I don't know. There is supposed to be a map of the hidden treasure, but you have to have better eyes than I have to see it."

"Did you take that cross rock to Alice?"

"Yes."

"Is it still in Alice?"

"Yes."

"Who went with you when you took it to Alice?"

"Jack Lawrence, Doc Noss and myself."

"Doc was with you?"

"He was always with me, just like a leech."

"You didn't try to get rid of him?"

"I didn't have reason to. I didn't have a chance to find out what kind of a man he was."

"I believe you testified you had around $5,000 invested in this venture?"

"Yes, sir."

"Back to this treasure, how much gold did Doc Noss tell you was there?"

"He said he had some engineer figure it out and there was approximately $162,000 worth of gold in there. That's a lot of gold."

"Did he ever show you any of that gold?"

"He showed me one bar in Alice that was supposed to be gold."

"Do you know if it was gold?"

"No, sir."

"Was it large or small?"

"No, it was a bar about so long about the size of a pound of gold."

The color of gold?"

"Yes, it was."

"You didn't have it assayed?"

"No."

"Did he ever show you any more of those bars?"

"No."

"Did anyone?"

"No, the Secret Service man in Albuquerque showed me a bar someone had sent him from Friona, Texas."

"You don't know whether Doc Noss had given it to the man in Friona, Texas or not?"

"I don't know anything about it."

"Was it after you saw this bar that you made the trip to Santa Fe with Doc Noss to see about getting a permit?"

"Well, I don't remember now, but I believe he showed me a bar afterwards, before we came to Santa Fe. When we first went to Santa Fe I wasn't going to be brought in this thing at all. I hadn't committed myself. All I was doing was furnishing an automobile and transportation. He wanted me to come with him and talk to these people. I told the attorney general in Santa Fe I had no interest in the treasure and didn't want any."

"In this mining venture you spoke of forming a corporation, but it wasn't formed?"

"No, the papers were drawn up, but that was the end of it."

"It was in your name, not in Doc Noss' name?"

"He told people he was working."

"Did he have any interest?"

"I agreed to give him half of what I might obtain."

"Were you paying him $800?"

"It amounted to that."

"What were you going to take as security?"

"All the claims were obtained in my name. Noss wouldn't have them in his. I told Noss I would give him half of whatever we got out of it, the two of us."

"Then, Mr. Ryan, you would have more interest in this mining venture than just putting up the money for Doc Noss?"

"As you put it, $2,000 or $3,000 is something you would want to be responsible for."

"Before you left Alice, before Doc Noss left Alice, had he mentioned anything about this treasure, this gold?"

"He certainly did. I got out of bed when I had this sprained ankle and we went to Santa Fe when there was snow on the ground, stayed there two days trying to obtain a permit."

"You went from Alice to Santa Fe?"

"We went to Friona, Texas, picked up Roscoe Parr, and drove on to Santa Fe on Sunday evening."

"Was he an associate in your business?"

"Roscoe Parr was the only man in New Mexico that Noss wanted me to have anything to do with."

"Do you know why?"

"I have never figured that out."

At some length and in considerable detail, Ryan was then led through the events of the day that culminated in the shooting.

He related he was on the porch when Noss came out of the house and started toward the truck. Asked how he knew Noss was going to the truck, Ryan replied, "He was walking in that direction and I took it for granted that was where he was going."

He said he rushed forward and set himself between Noss and the truck. "He had threatened my life and I told him to go back into the house and sit down until we got our business settled."

Ryan said he pulled his gun out of his pocket, whereupon Noss returned to the house, where, the witness said, Noss struck him. "The only thing I said to him after I got into the house was that I had found out from reliable citizens here that he was no good, that he had robbed these people and cheated them and that we were through and we were going back to Texas. That is when he knocked me through the window."

Gun in hand, Ryan said he went out onto the porch. In reply to a question, he said he did not know where his wife was at that time. "I was trying to keep Doc Noss

70

from getting to the truck.

"Did you say, 'Stop!'?"

"I did."

"Did you say, 'Get out from under there, you son-of-a bitch'?"

"No, sir, I said, 'Get up from there, you son-of-a bitch'. I thought he had fell down there to make me believe I had hit him, then he would jump up and go round and get his gun. After the first shot I hollered at him again. When I fired the second shot is when he fell."

"You don't recall anyone telling you to shoot him again?"

"No, sir, I don't. I won't say my wife didn't say that. I didn't hear it, and I wouldn't blame her if she did say it."

"What did you do after you fired the second shot and said, 'Get up from there'?"

"I never got any closer to the body than where this gentleman is. I walked back in the house, laid the gun on the drainboard and walked in and sat down, told them to call the sheriff and let them come out and arrest me."

"Did you know at the time you first went out in the yard and Noss came out after you, did you know at that time that Noss had the gun in the compartment of that car?"

"I hadn't seen it in there that morning, but I knew he always carried it there."

"You told him not to go out to the truck?"

"Yes."

"Why?"

"Because I didn't want him to get ahold of that gun. After he had threatened me why would I want him to go to the truck, get the gun and kill me?"

"Why didn't you send Jack Lawrence or Buck Harris for the gun after you went in the house?"

"Well, I hadn't thought of that. My thought was to get the law and to get the law to take him and the gun and put him in jail. I hadn't said anything to him about leaving until this accident occurred. I knew he was mean, I was afraid of him and I didn't want to discuss that with him until we was ready to leave."

"You didn't tell anybody to go after the law until after the shooting?"

"I didn't have time. I told him, 'I am going to send one of these boys to get the sheriff and send you to the penitentiary.' When I told him that, that is when he hit me on the chin, knocked me against the window, breaking the window. When I got back my balance I was at the end of the dining room."

"Were you afraid of Doc Noss?"

"Certainly I was afraid of him."

"Why did you hand the gun to Jack Lawrence, why didn't you keep it?"

"I didn't want to be standing up there talking to the man with a gun in my hand."

"If, as you say, Doc Noss said, 'I will kill every one of you', why didn't you lock the door?"

"How could I lock the back door when I had these five men out there to pay them off?"

The Court: "I don't think that is a proper question."

"We will withdraw that."

Ryan was then excused. The testimony was over.

The jury went into deliberation and a short time later returned a verdict of not guilty.

Ova did not speak favorably of the trial. She felt too little was made of the gold — "the real thing between them."

She told me, "Best that I can tell is that they got into a fight over the deal. Doc agreed to exchange gold bars for cash and Ryan would pay the money over at a certain spot at the missile range. The way they had it planned was like this — a plane would be flown in and the gold would be put on the plane and at the same time, Ryan would pay Doc in cash. I heard it was about $25,000. I was told Doc was to have the gold ready at the spot near where the plane was to land and when Ryan showed up and asked him where it was, Doc said the bars were in a hiding place nearby and he would bring them out as soon as he got his hands on the money. Well, Ryan said that he would not show the money until he saw the gold and the argument began, and the next thing anybody knew Doc was dead. Ryan had shot him with a pistol. It must have been a pretty violent argument because Doc was never the kind to hurt or threaten anyone. Oh, he would get a few drinks inside him and make a lot of noise, but he was really a nice man and he was harmless. I ought to know, I lived with him for fifteen years."

Mrs. Noss paused reflectively: "I think Ryan got hot over that gold. You read the trial transcript and you see almost nothing in it about the gold. They didn't want anything about the gold in the trial and they kept it out. Why? Well, your guess is as good as mine."

Members of the Noss family and friends looking into the shaft atop Victoria Peak (February 1953).

The inventory

Doc Noss was always certain that once the secret of his discovery became known, threats would be made upon his life. He had taken what he felt was the only course that made sense — removing the gold a few bars at a time from the caves and hiding them in crevices and faults nearby. Just how many bars were brought to the surface is not known; estimates range from less than a hundred to several thousand. A possible clue is contained in a somewhat conjectural inventory of Noss' possessions filed in the Probate Court of Dona Ana County following his death. Besides his interest in two mining projects in the Victoria Peak area, it listed certain personal items, including the following:

One metal steamer trunk containing papers, documents, books, maps, and other miscellaneous items, held by the United States Government, Secret Service Agent, Albuquerque, N.M. for investigation.

One metal strong box, containing documents, papers and miscellaneous items, also being held by U.S. Secret Agent, Albuquerque;

Three bars of metal, believed to be held by the U. S. Mint in Denver, said to have been receipted for, to MILTON E. NOSS, in the amount of approximately $90,000.00 since 1940 or 1941.

Fifty-one (51) bars of metal, of undetermined value or content, believed to be in possession of the U. S. Government Agent in Albuquerque, together with the above named three bars, pending investigation and evaluation.

Two bars of metal, presumably in Del Rio, Texas, at the Val Verde National Bank. Value not known.

One bar of metal, said to be in Grand Junction, Colorado, or Colorado Springs, Colorado, probably now in the hands of United States government.

One suitcase, not found, presumed to contain legal documents, metal bars, gems and or samples, trinkets, and other miscellaneous items. This may have been a metal strong box having two padlocks. These and other items are presumed to be in the hands of U. S. Secret Service department.

Two bars of metal, presumably in a bank in Phoenix, Arizona.

The inventory bore the signature, "Merle Horzmann, Administratrix."

Now alone, Mrs. Noss did not have the means to accomplish the task to which she had set herself: reopening the shaft. Money would be needed for equipment and help, but a more urgent item at the moment was food to sustain herself and the family during the long hours on Victoria Peak. There were more to feed now that her sons and daughters took turns working on the peak. She took part-time jobs in nearby towns, waiting tables or playing the piano. Occasionally friends loaned her small amounts of money in return for the promise of a fraction of interest in whatever of value might ultimately be removed from the caverns.

In her renewal of mining permits in the years following Noss' death, Ova discovered that Mrs. Violet Noss was making inquiries as to Ova's right to the permits. Apprehensive, Ova prevailed upon Guy Shepard, the then Commissioner of Public Lands, to issue a "To Whom It May Concern" letter. It read in part: "Mrs. Ova M. Noss is the only Mrs. Noss who has had any contact with the State Land Office during my administration

... Our records do not disclose any rights to any other Mrs. Noss who may have purported to be the wife of the late Dr. M. E. Noss by a subsequent marriage."

The stipulations of condemnation between the State of New Mexico and the federal government did not, at first, pose much of a threat to Ova Noss. She felt reasonably secure even as she saw prospectors and farmers leave the area in considerable numbers by order of the Department of the Army. Victoria Peak was not within the condemned area and it appeared the Noss claim might escape the mandate to cease and desist. Mrs. Noss, with the occasional help of a few friends, worked long hours, sometime far into the night. Occasionally, they interrupted their excavation efforts to search for another entrance to the caverns.

One day Ova received a notice from the U. S. Defense Department advising that Victoria Peak has been added to the acreage under lease by the Army. It directed her to leave Victoria Peak and take whatever steps she felt appropriate to protect her mining permit.

Ova ignored the order.

Sometime later she received a similar demand from the State of New Mexico. This she also ignored.

Her next move was to call upon a U. S. Senator from New Mexico, Dennis Chaves, for help. On December 3, 1952, Senator Chaves wrote a letter to Brig. Gen. G. G. Eddy, the Commander at the White Sands Proving Grounds (the name adopted by the government for the condemned area):

This letter will introduce the bearer Mrs. Noss who has a State Prospector's Permit on certain lands lying within the Alamogordo bombing range under your jurisdiction and direction.

I do not happen to know Mrs. Noss personally but this matter was brought to my attention by very dear friends of mine whom I have known for many years.

General, it is my understanding that there are certain minerals in the area that should be explored being consistent within your operation and at the same time looking for the better interest of our country.

I would appreciate anything you can do in behalf of Mrs. Noss so that she may further her plans and ideas.

In the same period, Ova prevailed upon Senator Clinton P. Anderson also to write General Eddy. General Eddy ruled out any further operations by Mrs. Noss or anyone else, stating that the necessary papers were being prepared to transfer to the federal government "all rights pertaining to minerals on the land comprising the White Sands Proving Grounds."

The state-federal controversy appeared to center on interpretations of one of the lease provisions. The Army insisted it was entitled to use not only the surface of the ground, but also to supervise all mineral and mining activities.

The state's response: Not so, the Army's jurisdiction is restricted solely to the surface.

The dispute finally reached federal court in a friendly suit. The ruling was a sort of compromise: The Army was entitled to use only the surface and, secondly, no person may enter the Missile Range without the Army's approval, whether to mine, prospect or farm.

The grant of power to the Army to keep people off the base was logical, but worked to the considerable disadvantage of claimants to the Victoria Peak treasure; it was all the more aggravating because they had a sympathetic ear at the State Land Office.

Even though distressed by Ova's refusal to leave the area, the Army was not yet prepared to resort to sterner measures, unwilling to bring its power to bear publicly against the poor, yet aggressive, widow from Clovis, New

Mexico.

The Land Office advised the White Sands command in trenchant language that it felt Mrs. Noss was within her rights to remain there until the expiration of her current annual permit. There were further exchanges, including a threat by the Land Office to go to court to help Mrs. Noss complete her work on the peak. But that meant allowing her to remain for an indeterminate period.

The confrontation between the two powers did not produce anything tangible at that stage, but it added strength to the Noss family's determination to stay at the peak, even though formal condemnation proceedings were completed. Little did the Army realize it would have Ova on its hands for another three years, marked by a series of letters from senators and governors with various requests on Ova's behalf. Most of the pleas suggested it would be wise for the Army to reconsider its refusal and allow her to find and remove what her late husband had discovered.

It was all to no avail. Ova left the peak in the summer of 1955. Federal marshals politely and firmly walked her to an armored vehicle, each flanking her in soldierly fashion.

It would be her last view of Victoria Peak for more than a decade but it would not be the Army's last view of Ova Noss.

The first salvo beyond the gates of White Sands came a few months later, set in motion by a group friendly to Ova. The leader was Gordon Bjornson, then of Brady, Texas. Bjornson appeared at the Land Office with a written statement expressing the group's willingness to attempt entry into the mountain "regardless of cost until this job is finished." It said his associates had more than $50,000 available for the operation and asked for permission to visit the peak to observe whether there were any unusual technical problems that would make the project inadvisable.

Surprisingly, General Eddy agreed to allow the group to schedule not only one inspection but a second later on. But prior to entering the grounds, the group found itself at odds as to whether to excavate the shaft or try to find another entry into the caverns.

At this point, official silence enveloped the arrangement. White Sands did not respond to requests by either Bjornson or the Land Office. In desperation, Bjornson wrote the then Secretary of Defense, Robert A. Lovett, expressing "great faith in Mrs. Noss." He stated his group would be willing to try to obtain permission of *both* the federal and state governments, promising that "the entire undertaking can be finished within approximately ninety days," working under the direction of the commander. The letter further stated Noss removed from the caverns "about eighty-six bars of gold, a statue of the Virgin Mary of pure gold, a jeweled crown, Spanish swords and other relics of Spanish origin . . ."

Nothing came of Bjornson's efforts. The Army and the Land Office could agree on only one aspect: Bjornson or anyone else must obtain the consent of both government offices.

The state office said it was willing to issue a permit.

In a courteous denial, White Sands insisted that to allow Bjornson onto the range would set a precedent adverse to the Army's primary objective, missile testing.

While Ova and associates were thus seeking official consent to return to the peak, another drama was unfolding at White Sands — one that would ultimately reach into the tight, autocratic confines of the Pentagon.

Its significance would be startling and persuasive, strongly supporting the truth of Noss' claims.

In 1958 four men, two actively in the military service, came upon a cave at Victoria Peak. If they were looking for the Noss caverns it was more to satisfy their curiosity

— having heard so much about the Noss find — than to engage in any serious exploration.

The two servicemen were Capt. Leonard V. Fiege and Tom Berlett, both of the U. S. Air Force. Fiege was stationed at the time at Holloman Air Force base at nearby Alamogordo. Berlett may have been in a retired status then. Their companions were civilians.

What they saw that November day is contained in an affidavit prepared and signed by Captain Fiege, reading in its entirety as follows:

We had separated and I went down a canyon by myself. I saw this small hill and open caves. I climbed the hill and found a small cave that was fairly well hidden.

I was to meet the other boys at the base of the hill but they had not yet arrived, so I decided to go into this cave and look around.

The cave was large enough to stand up in until I came to a small opening about 30 inches around. I shined my light into this hole and it looked like it opened up into a large shaft on the other end.

I climbed through on my stomach and entered the large part of the shaft again. This shaft led into the main cavern. The dust was so thick and the air was foul and hard to breathe, so I sat down on what I thought was a dust covered pile of rocks.

I was a little sick and was going to get out of there as soon as I stopped coughing. The dust fell off the pile I was sitting on and I started inspecting this area.

The pile of so-called rocks was not rocks but smelted gold in bars about the size of a house brick. I realized what I had found and grew a little excited. I wanted to explore more of this area but in my excitement I moved too fast and the dust started flying.

With my flashlight I saw three piles of this gold

all lined up and another pile off to the left that was partly covered by the wall of the cave that had fallen in.

In trying to shine the light around the cave to see if there were any more stacks of this around, I found it almost impossible to see farther than about 15 to 20 feet because of the dust in the air. It was like headlights on a car shining into dense fog.

I started getting sick again and made my way back out. I was determined to take the boys back with me when they came to this hill.

I was dirty and sick when they arrived. I told them what I had found and we agreed to go in and look at it again. We got as far as the small opening together but Ken and Mil were too large to get through so Tom Berlett and I went in alone.

The dust we walked in after we slid through this tunnel was about five inches deep and we stirred a lot of it up. We went in to these four piles of gold and confirmed the findings.

We got sick again and moved back out of the tunnel and talked to the other boys. Tom and I handled the gold and thought about taking some of it out, but decided against it because we were not familiar with laws that governed the claiming of this gold.

We might lose it all if we took it out now, so we decided to go back in and cover this area up so nobody could find it. If we could find it, so could other people with enough nerve to go back in this cave past the small passageway.

We decided the best thing to do was to close off this entrance with rocks and dirt. Tom and I re-entered this cave and worked for about 3½ hours off and on between going back to the small tunnel to get air. We caved in the roof and walls to make it look like the tunnel came to a dead-end. Then we *left.*

We have tried many ways to get into this area to remove the gold but we were always refused by the commander of the range.

I believe that with gas masks or some air filtering device we can work in the shaft with little difficulty. If more of this shaft has caved in, other than what we did ourselves, it will take time to remove this so we can get a clear passage to recover this gold.

The piles were about four feet across the bottom and about three feet high in triangle shaped piles. Because of the dust, we did not see any more but we believe that there is much more in the area.

We could string lights and run air into the cave once we get through our cave-in. This would give us a chance to find any other treasure that might be in there with the four piles that we saw.

Fiege may have indeed stumbled onto one of the Noss treasure caches, either in the main treasure room or hidden in another cave selected by Noss after the collapse of the main shaft.

At any rate, after his decision to block off the entrance to the cave, and resisting the considerable temptation to remove a bar or two from the cavern, Fiege went to the Judge Advocate's office at Holloman, and there disclosed the nature of his find to the head of the office, Col. Sigmund I. Gasiewicz.

Gasiewicz was intensely interested in what Fiege was saying but, understandably, doubts filled his mind. Over at White Sands was a separate and distinct command with the usual inter-service jealousies and competition. He might have wished Fiege had found the gold at Holloman. He put aside an initial impulse to let Fiege escort him to Victoria Peak for a first-hand inspection. That would require an Army permit, perhaps even a series of hearings.

What seemed wise at the moment to Colonel Gasie-wicz's legally trained mind was a procedure that would put the state on notice. He telephoned the Land Office in Santa Fe, and talked to Oscar Jordan, then Land Office attorney. His disclosure was cautiously succinct, to the effect that there was an Air Force captain in his office who had found a gold bar on the White Sands Missile Range. He asked what disposition should be made of it. Jordan advised that the gold be turned over to a federal agency, either the Treasury department in Washington or the Secret Service office in Albuquerque.*

Captain Fiege, his companions at the time of the discovery and Colonel Gasiewicz met to discuss what steps should be taken.

They decided on this outline:

Form a corporation "to protect what we have found," take the matter through the appropriate military channels in Washington, and there make formal application for permission to re-enter the Missile Range and retrieve the gold. At that point they thought all they would need was a permit from the Army. Surely the State of New Mexico (the owner of the land and landlord to the tenant Army) would have no interest in this effort to take possession of something of value which they had found and was legally theirs.

Fiege, Berlett and Gasiewicz proceeded hopefully to the Pentagon. There they contacted officials in the Treasury and Defense departments. They did not expect, nor did they receive, an open-arms reception. The government was in the midst of a project set at the

---

*Later, Jordan would reduce the conversation to a memo and place it in a file, open to public inspection. From the memo it appears Jordan was under the impression Fiege had brought a gold bar into the JAG office. However, Gasiewicz subsequently would deny this, saying Fiege came into his office empty-handed, contending he (Gasiewicz) saw no gold bar then or later.

highest national priority, involving the testing of the first atom bomb at a spot called Trinity Site, and in no mood to wrestle with the parody of a lost gold treasure legend, or with a request to lift the ban against non-military activities at White Sands.

The petitioners soon found themselves in a bureaucratic maze of exasperatingly slow movement through the intricate network of authority, a way of life in the Pentagon.

Whatever the reason, the pace became a crawl. Months passed. Finally, late in 1961, three years after Fiege's disclosure, the Army agreed to allow the exploration. The various offices were notified, and preparations went forward for the assembling of a military work crew, with proper equipment, to go onto Victoria Peak.

What spurred the negotiations along was something known only to a few at the time — lie-detector tests administered to Fiege and Berlett by order of the Treasury department. The tests indicated both men were telling the truth about their discovery of gold. This naturally strengthened Gasiewicz's position and bound the group more closely in the determination to see the project through.

No announcement was made of the impending exploration at the peak. The State of New Mexico was kept in the dark, either by design or through carelessness. In all respects, secrecy was the order of the day.

For a number of years four friends of the Noss family — Ray D. Bradley, Robert H. Bradley, H. L. Moreland and R. B. Gray — had occasionally visited the Noss family at Victoria Peak, sometimes lending a hand. Even after the Army took over, they continued the visits, but much less frequently of course and with greater care so as to avoid detection.

On this particular fall night in 1961 they set out again, having parked their car at a discreet distance from the range boundary. They climbed a fence and headed toward the peak some several hours away by foot. A full moon shed friendly light on the uneven terrain. They were in no hurry; it was a mission with no special goal.

They reached the basin at daybreak, approaching the higher slopes of Victoria peak from a westerly direction. There were unusual noises and, they thought, voices emanating beyond a ridge just ahead. They moved to the top and peered over. A short distance away, less than fifty yards, were men and equipment at and just below the Noss shaft, busily engaged in a digging operation. (They had no way of knowing it was the Fiege exploration being conducted under military supervision).

Their intent — and startled — gaze sorted out several pieces of equipment, including a military jeep, a weapons carrier, two light plants, one running; several 5-gallon G. I. gasoline cans, a walkie-talkie, mining wedges and heavy shoring timber, light-plant cables leading into a deep cleft. Several men were using hand shovels to enlarge a hole a few feet below the peak's summit.

With friend Ova Noss in mind, one with a camera in hand took several photos, some of which turned out to be sharp enough to record the identifying number of the military jeep - C987C57.

Deciding to move out from behind the ridge and within view of the work party, they were met by an Army officer (a Captain Swanner) who brusquely demanded to know what they were doing there. He ordered them to leave, saying the area was classified and they should be thankful he did not put them under arrest. There was no attempt at apology. They turned about, returned to Alamogordo and promptly telephoned Mrs. Noss to relate what they had seen.

The confrontation

The news from Bradley and companions was more than enough to incite Ova Noss to action. Clovis townfolk were quite familiar with her habit of adventuring forth in the small hours of the night, often in chase of some vague report or bit of speculation related to the treasure trove.

But here was no idle speculation. She knew and trusted the Bradleys; they had seen the military on top of *her* peak and she was going to find out why they were there.

She called son Harold to come to Clovis at once, then hurried over to the office of a lawyer friend, Dan Buzzard.

With Ova on an extension, Buzzard telephoned Oscar Jordan at Santa Fe for advice on what move the Noss family should make.

Jordan urged Ova to put the entire matter in the hands of the Land Office. He would meet with his superiors the next day to decide what steps to take.

That sounded all too slow for Ova; patience was not a virtue in matters relating to the treasure.

Harold arrived in Clovis the following morning after an all-night drive. Immediately the two, with daughter Letha, motored to Holloman Air Force base headquarters. Refusing to be put off, they were granted a meeting that afternoon with a Colonel Thomason of the Judge Advocate's office. The Colonel said he had no knowledge of any activity at the peak and ridiculed the whole idea of the existence of a gold trove anywhere in the area.

Inasmuch as the incident in question had taken place at the White Sands Missile Range he suggested they contact a Colonel Jaffe of the Judge Advocate office there.

The meeting with Jaffe on the following day was marked by moments of angry tension. The visitors found Jaffe openly cynical. He brushed aside their claims about a discovery of gold, insisted it was all a myth, and denied there had been any digging at Victoria Peak by the military. When Ova asked him to permit them to inspect the peak area personally, Jaffe said that would not be possible; a permit would have to come from the Commandant's office, and in the event they made such a request, he, Jaffe, would vigorously oppose it because of the peak's location in the heart of a prime impact area.

The following hours and days were busy ones for the Noss family and counsel:

3 p.m., Nov. 2, 1961: Marvin Beckwith returns to Clovis. The following morning be meets with Mr. Florsheim and Mr. Jordan of the Land Office in Santa Fe. Florsheim says he had made preparations to leave by airplane to investigate the matter but the Commissioner questioned whether or not the State had an interest that would permit it to get involved. Beckwith said the four men who had seen military personnel working on Victoria Peak were prepared to sign affidavits to that effect. Jordan and Florsheim seem most concerned and feel Mrs. Noss should be given every opportunity to protect her interests and that the Air Force should be stopped immedi-

ately. Mr. Jordan requested that the affidavits be furnished him as quickly as possible and that they would pursue the matter even if it meant "shaking up the powers at both the Holloman and White Sands bases."

In order to give the state a basis for involvement, it was agreed Mrs. Noss would grant the State a 5% interest in the treasure trove. It was felt by both Florsheim and Jordan that, subject to approval from the federal government, a 120-day permit could be arranged to allow Mrs. Noss to return to the peak.

Nov. 4: Beckwith drives to Clovis and acquaints Dan Buzzard with the results of the meeting with Jordan and Florsheim. They summon H. Moreland, R. B. Gray, Ray Bradley and Bob Bradley to Clovis.

Nov. 5: All four men complete affidavits in Buzzard's office. Buzzard also prepares a letter from Mrs. Noss to the State assigning a 5% interest in the treasure trove found on Section 16, Township 16 South, Range 3 East.

Nov. 6: Marvin and Ova return to Santa Fe and furnish the Land Office with the affidavits and the letter. Florsheim calls Lt. Col. Morton S. Jaffe and asks him about Army personnel working on the Noss mine. Col. Jaffe replies he investigated after Beckwith and Mrs. Noss had been to his office, that personally he had found no Army personnel doing any type of work on the mine and that no treasure had been exposed. Then Florsheim told the Colonel his investigation was inadequate or that someone was lying about the whole matter. The Colonel said, "What business is it of the State to be prying into the matter?" Florsheim replied the State had a 5% interest in the case, read him excerpts from one of the affidavits, and asked if he wanted him to read any more. Jaffe said, "No, that's sufficient. I will check further."

Later in the afternoon a Mr. Shadel of the Corps of Engineers in Albuquerque informs Florsheim that there had been activity at the Noss location and that White Sands officials were aware of it. Florsheim told him he was going to call in the FBI and Mr. Shadel stated, "For God's sake don't do anything until I have talked to you." Florsheim agreed he would not take any action until he and Shadel could meet.

Nov. 6:   Ova Noss and Harold Beckwith leave for Wichita, Kansas, to engage an attorney to represent them.

There was now accumulating evidence to support the fact of the discovery of a gold cache by Fiege and Berlett as the news of the positive Fiege lie-detector tests reached the claimants.

A few days later official curiosity at Santa Fe was further aroused with confirmation that Colonel Gasiewicz (according to a Land Office memo dated Nov. 7, signed by Florsheim) "had gone to Washington with Captain Fiege and contacted the Treasurer of the United States and the Director of Mints and explained to them their discovery of treasure trove, that both had then contacted the Secretary of the Army and asked for help in uncovering the treasure."

It was no surprise to the Noss family. They had consistently, at times passionately, pressed for the truth of their claims. Now a somewhat official military stamp appeared to have been placed by the Fiege and Gasiewicz moves. It occurred to the family that the Army had been diligent in following up on the Fiege discovery by conducting its own probe at the site. No problem at all. Just go out there with equipment and start digging. But how difficult to obtain the Army's consent for a mere inspection by the Nosses, let alone a reasonable time to explore.

In the months to come Ova Noss, not exactly the reticent type, would proclaim her suspicions to friends — that one or more of the clusters of gold bars that Doc hid in crevices near the peak had been found by the military, removed from the base and sold. Subsequent events would strengthen her belief and cause her to wonder how long the Defense department and the Army could hold off the increasing demands for re-entry.

Unfortunately, there were not many "public" pressures at the moment. The newspapers had not yet smelled out the Fiege discovery; the entire affair would be dormant on a national basis until the day when the subject of the treasure would surface under more distinguished auspices — the Watergate testimony before the Irvin committee. But that was a few years away.

Letters and memos continued to flow back and forth between federal and state officials, punctuated by meetings in Albuquerque, Santa Fe and Washington. None produced a plan for re-entry.

Left to right, Noss counsel Bob Martin of Wichita, Kansas, Ova Noss, and counsel Phil Koury.

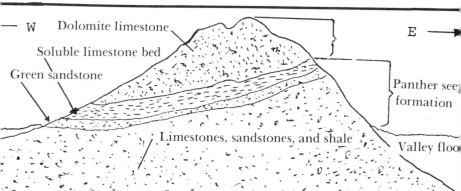

Geologic cross section of Victoria Peak.

Ova has counsel

In Wichita Ova Noss and Marvin concluded their search for an attorney, spent a good part of the morning of November 7 acquainting Robert Martin with their story. One of the most distinguished trial attorneys in the midwest, Martin knew Marvin Beckwith from prior representations in matters involving oil rights, a field in which the attorney was an acknowledged expert.

But this was his first awareness of the treasure trove matter. His was a busy schedule with little time for cases outside his field, let alone controversies over treasures, lost or in being. And especially one that appeared to require some kind of immediate legal action — a conclusion drawn quickly by the attorney as he listened to Mrs. Noss relate the circumstances of the Army's mining activities spied on by her four friends.

Finally, Martin told them he would be willing to maintain a personal interest in their situation but, with time forbidding, was not able to handle the case. However, he said, he was acquainted with a Kansas City, Missouri, attorney who might agree to accept their case.

Martin called my office late that afternoon and drew from me a consent to listen to Ova Noss. If I agreed to represent her he promised he would make himself available to help as co-counsel and take part in any major moves which I deemed advisable. He said the Nosses were virtually without funds but would advance $500 to cover expenses of what appeared to be a logical first move — a trip to White Sands Missile Range for a visit with the commanding office, Brig. Gen. John Shinkle, specifically to question him on the Army's unauthorized digging and to check into the Fiege discovery.

Ova and Marvin were in my office the next day, November 8, 1961, with high expectations. She did not hesitate to express her disappointment over my admission that I had never heard of Doc's fabulous discovery.

At first glance, one might not expect quick and spirited movement in a person of her size; Ova Noss was as vivacious as a satyr. With her noisy sense of humor, her ready invectives against enemies ("the rats are stealing me blind at Victoria Peak"), it was readily apparent to the listener that a very sharp and aggressive spirit lurked in that active brain. I did not dare ask but I guessed her age to be in the late 60's or early 70's, though it might have been a perfectly safe inquiry. One would have been hard put not to feel on a very friendly basis with her immediately.

An occasional invective, spoken easily, fell ever so lightly on the ear. (Once she called at 2 a.m.: "Koury, get your ass out here to Clovis. Big things are happening." Of the military at White Sands: "The whole lot of them ain't worth a hoot in hell"). She had had little education in the conventional sense, but in many ways exhibited a remarkable wisdom. Many times in the decade and a half of our acquaintance I watched her devitalize opposing arguments and convert them to her cause. Her personal dynamism actually fascinated people, sensing a compassionate nature behind her convulsive drive, explosive fervor and reckless contempt for obstacles. Once I advised her, with as much professional gravity as seemed appropriate, that it might be advisable for her to stop selling additional fractions of her legal interest in the treasure without first determining how much of an interest she had left. "Ova," I said, attempting a fatherly tone, "one should not sell more than one owns." She smiled, "Everyone will get something and we will all be happy."

I had broached the matter of compensation for legal services to Ova a number of times. Obviously she was not in a position to manage even a small retainer, much less reimburse us for travel and other expenses. Robert Martin and I came to view labors on behalf of Ova as a sort of dedication, leaving to the gods the highly speculative possibility of sharing in the treasure itself.

In a letter agreement which I prepared, Ova happily assigned to us a 5 percent interest in whatever came out of the caverns and an additional 5 percent of whatever monies she derived from percentage sales of her interest or from any other source. Though the arrangement fell far short of reason or logic, the thought of abandoning the gasconading housewife from Clovis never entered our minds. After a few years, Martin made himself available only in an advisory role and ultimately he separated himself from the project entirely. His share, 2½ percent, was assigned to me by Ova. When an associate, George O'Laughlin, entered the case I assigned him 2 percent of my 5 percent interest.

General Shinkle's greeting was friendly, with much less reserve than we expected. He beckoned Robert Martin and me to chairs in front of his massive desk, saying he would call in Lt. Col. Morton Jaffe of the Judge Advocate office. Jaffe entered stiffly, unsmiling. The amenities were barely over when Jaffe bluntly announced his position on the Noss treasure discovery — "a fake and a myth". Shinkle's reaction was a trace of a smile, apparently for the moment wishing to keep matters on an affable basis. It soon became apparent we had not come prepared to show him documentary evidence of certain basic facts and occurrences involving military personnel. We had assumed the General would have been so briefed by his own staff.

We told him there were witnesses who saw Army or Air Force personnel at the peak recently, using military equipment in an excavation operation.

The General shook his head. "There has been no activity there."

Bob and I exchanged glances, no doubt thinking the same thought: Surely the General was made aware of the Pentagon's preparations for the work party led by Fiege. How could the operation have taken place without his approval?

We then produced the photographs taken by Bradley at the scene and placed them on the desk. Shinkle studied each one carefully, showing no vestige of surprise.

"If there was digging going on out there it was not with my knowledge," he said. "And you can be sure it will be stopped immediately if it's still going on."

This treasure trove business, the General said softly, has been a source of considerable trouble and perplexity to the government.

"We've wasted a lot of man-hours," he said. "It has taken operating and command personnel to police the area. We had to do that in order to guard against injury to trespassers, handle the innumerable requests of your clients and others. Gentlemen, we are a vital testing ground in the national interest and obviously have no time for chasing after lost gold or whatever."

We brought up the names of Leonard V. Fiege, Air Force captain and pilot, and Thomas F. Berlett, both stationed at nearby Holloman Air Force base. Our information, we said, was that they had found a substantial number of gold bars, maybe 100, and this find had been reported to the U. S. Treasury department.

He shook his head, a grin on his face.

"Nothing to it," he said. Nor was he impressed by my disclosure that the Treasury department had administered lie detector tests to Fiege and Berlett and the tests supported the truth of their discovery.

Martin and I left the missile range convinced it was

95

not a good meeting. General Shinkle's polite offers of cooperation — "within the rules and limitations of the range" — and Jaffe's cynical remarks made it seem quite unlikely that the Army would grant the permission we were seeking, entry upon Victoria Peak by a member of the Noss family or a representative. True, Shinkle had maintained an official posture throughout the meeting but Martin and I were in agreement that he shared Jaffe's opinion that Doc Noss was a faker and a fraud.

Before departing, we assured the General we would prepare a lengthy letter setting out those aspects of the case which we are in a position to document or prove through witnesses. Shinkle said he would look forward to the letter inasmuch as there probably was much in the Noss case not known to him.

Bob Martin returned to Wichita and I went to Santa Fe to keep an appointment with Joseph Andregg, who had worked for Doc Noss at Victoria Peak and was on the scene the day the dynamiting collapsed the shaft entrance.

At the time of our meeting, he was an electrician at Los Alamos, birthplace of the atom bomb, in a job that required a thorough check of his background prior to the granting of a security clearance. I had undertaken a search to determine his whereabouts without knowing whether he was in New Mexico. Random inquiries among some Spanish-American families in Santa Fe had produced an address. In a telephone call to his home Andregg confirmed his prior relationship with Doc Noss.

Andregg commuted between Santa Fe and Los Alamos, and when he came to my room in the La Fonda hotel that November evening he was wearing work clothes and a Los Alamos security badge with photograph and identification number.

A pleasant, soft-spoken person, about 40 years old,

Andregg was not given to over-statement, as I soon learned in the course of our taped conversation.

"Mr. Andregg, did you work with Doc Noss at Victoria Peak?"

"Yes, for about 2 years."

"Did you ever go down into the shaft itself with him?"

"Yes, but not all the way."

"Did you ever enter the rooms where he said he found certain treasures?"

"No, just down to the first level."

"First level?"

He smiled, "That's as far as he wanted me to go. There was a rock ledge about forty feet down."

"What did you ever see him bring up from the treasure rooms?"

"A lot of things. One time I saw some small canvas bags with articles in them."

"What kind of articles?"

"Well, they were heavy, and there was some bars that I had seen."

"Do you have reason to believe they were valuable?"

"Yes."

"How do you know?"

"Well, they were gold."

"Did you ever see him cut into these bars or scratch them in such a way to indicate that they were gold?"

"Yes."

"Did he ever tell you they were gold bars?"

"Yes."

"What did you see in the way of treasures other than gold?

"Well, there were gold coins and a sword and a crown and several small articles."

"Generally, what did he do with these things?"

"Well, he would take them out and I would go back to the camp and he would go off with them, I don't know where."

"Did you suspect that he was hiding them somewhere in the area?"

"Yes."

"Was there any occasion when you accompanied him on one of these missions when he had a large number of these bars?"

"I was there when he moved forty bars."

"Tell me about it."

"Well, we was coming down a canyon and he says, 'You wait with the horses here and I'll be back'."

"Did you see the forty bars?"

"No, he told me about them."

"How was it that you went to work for Noss?"

"I was working about eight miles from the peak, on my uncle's ranch."

"How old were you at the time?"

"About 15 or 16."

"Do you have a vivid recollection of the mine and the things you saw?"

"Yes."

"Is is hard for you to remember the events?"

"Some of them. It's hard but some of them I remember."

"But you feel perfectly sure about the gold?"

"Oh, yes."

"No question in your mind that it was gold?"

"No."

"Do you know or have you heard of a man named Farnsworth?"

"Yes."

"In what connection?"

"He was there at the mine, I think about three weeks, and he took some of the stuff for assay."

"What do you mean, some of the stuff?"

"I think some gold bars."

"Why do you say 'think'? Gold is the only thing they could assay."

"Actually, I just heard them talk about it. He said he was going to take some stuff in for assay."

"Did you ever hear anything more with reference to the assay?"

"No."

"Where did they take it, do you know?"

"I think Silver City."

"Was there an assay office there?"

"Yes."

"Did you ever go with Noss in connection with the articles or metal that he took from the mine?"

"Well, we went to El Paso in a Ford pick-up and he had a lot of these articles in there, in the pick-up."

"Including swords and bars of gold?"

"Yes."

"Anything else that you can remember?"

"Well, there was saddles and medals and suitcases and stuff like that."

Andregg described a trip to El Paso in Noss' truck, both checking into the El Paso Del Norte hotel.

"I stayed all night there and Doc left. He didn't show up that night. The next morning he come in with $1,500 in travelers checks."

"How did you know it amounted to $1,500?"

"He showed it to me."

"In other words, you think he must have gotten rid of some of the treasures and that was what he sold them for?"

"I believe so."

"There has been mention of a crown in the pick-up truck. Did you see a silver or a gold crown that was part of the articles you took to El Paso?"

"Yes."

"Was it silver or gold?"

"I believe it was gold."

"And did it have a cross on top?"

"Yes."

"And was there a jewel in the cross?"

"Yes."

"And do you think it, too, came from the mine?"

"I believe so."

I asked whether there was any question in his mind that Noss was removing those articles from the mine.

"I know he was."

"You're perfectly sure about it?"

"Yes."

"Did you ever see him remove any gold coins from the mine?"

"Yes."

"What kind of coins?"

"Well, just old coins."

"In great numbers?"

"Yes."

"Would he fill his canvas bag with coins alone, and would you assist him in moving this material up the shaft from the point where you were stationed?"

"He wouldn't fill the bag because if it was full he couldn't of carried it."

"Mr. Andregg, the records show that Noss discovered this mine in 1937. When did you first go to work for him?"

"In 1941 up to the middle of 1943."

"And you were there regularly?"

"Yes, except when I did a chore for my uncle eight miles away."

"What is your uncle's name?"

"Frank Andregg."

"Did you tell your uncle about the mine and what Noss was doing when you first went to work there?"

"Yes, I did."

"Did Noss and your uncle ever get together and talk about the treasure?"

"Yes."

"And you heard these conversations about the mine

between the two men?"

"Right."

"Was Noss free in telling him about details of his operation?"

Andregg paused. He said Noss only mentioned that he had found gold. "He didn't tell anybody anything in detail."

"He wasn't telling what it was he had taken out of the mine?"

"That's right."

Not unusual in interrogations by lawyers, I had prepared a question to test Andregg's memory, possibly his veracity. I knew he had not seen any of the Nosses since the dynamite blast (except Mrs. Noss in passing one day, several years prior to our meeting). If, as he asserts, he was at the peak working for Noss he must have known about or observed the cave-in. A minor detail of that incident — Doc Noss irately chasing the engineer down the hillside, a shoe in hand — was the basis of my attempt at entrapment.

I began with a reference to the dynamiting:

"As you know, Noss tried to widen the opening at the base of the shaft. He wanted to do this to make it easier to squeeze through. So he took an engineer down there, and the engineer planted too large a charge of dynamite and the shaft caved in. Now, were you there that day?"

"Yes, I was at the bottom of the mountain on the other side from where the entrance of the shaft is. I was bringing up some material."

"And about how far away were you from the top of the peak?"

"I'd say about a half mile."

"And what did you hear?"

"Well, I heard the dynamite go off and I saw the rocks fly."

"Up in the air, above the shaft?

"Yes."

"Can you describe the sound?"

"It was just like a . . . . just like a boom, like dynamite going off."

"Then what?"

"Well, him and this engineer, there was hard feelings."

"What happened?"

"Doc Noss chased the engineer down the mountainside."

"Tell me about it."

"Well, Doc had his shoe in his hand and he was plenty mad."

As he prepared to leave my hotel room in Santa Fe, the recording device having been turned off, Andregg volunteered a few more details about the trip with Noss to El Paso. He said Noss stopped the truck as they were leaving Hembrillo basin, walked some distance to a low ridge, removed a heavy foot locker from a hiding place, dragged it to the truck and lifted it onto the truck bed. That box, Andregg recalled, was not in the truck the next morning. The youth assumed Noss had sold the contents, hence the $1,500 in travelers checks.

Chester Johnson of the New Mexico Museum had no knowledge of my interview with Andregg. Two years later, Johnson talked with Andregg about his employment with Noss. In a report to the museum, Johnson characterized Andregg as a person who "cared nothing for the gold but greatly admired Noss and his fancy black western outfit." The report continues: "At the nearby camp outside the cave Andregg helped saw a bar into quarters. This bar was soft and could be bent. He knows the bar was neither copper nor brass."

The report also made reference to a meeting at the camp between Noss and an unidentified man: "The man asked Noss if he had 'the crown'. Noss replied, 'Right here,' and slid a satchel across the table to him. The man opened the satchel and a sack inside the satchel, and peered into it. He seemed satisfied as he closed the sack and returned the satchel. Andregg never saw the crown since it was not his business to see it."

The 1977 exploration. An MP watches members of the crew from Stanford University institute string wire and devices in preparation for radar soundings atop Victoria Peak.

Army military police at base of the Peak. Mrs. Noss is partly visible at the right.

Military stone-walling?

Robert Martin's letter to General John Shinkle was concise and direct. Its eight pages, single spaced, made clear our concern over the behavior and attitude of the military toward the Noss interests. It singled out Colonel Jaffe's statement on November 6 to the effect he was not aware of military-conducted operations at the peak.

The letter continues:

Beckwith, Ova Noss and Charles Laird called on Col. Jaffe. When questioned about the discovery of certain treasures from the Noss mine and the work that was being done by military personnel on the Noss mine, Col. Jaffe denied both queries. He stated that he had been on the base a year and that nothing had been exposed in the like of a treasure or minerals on the White Sands Air Force Base and that there was definitely no mining or sub-surface work being done by military personnel. He stated that the Army was not in the mining business. He also denied inquiries from the Land Office pertaining to this matter. During the conversation he seemed extremely familiar with the Noss mine and its location. When asked if it would be possible to arrange for a personal inspection, escorted or otherwise, Col. Jaffe emphatically stated that it would be impossible; however, it would be at the discretion of the General, but he would not recommend same, and especially not on that particular day due to concentrated testing in that area.

Martin's letter pointed to the fact that Ova Noss, though possessing an unexpired mining permit, was "summarily ejected" from the land by officers in charge.

"They were not compensated, nor was their property made the subject of any condemnation proceeding. At the time they were forced off the property the Nosses, on the advice of officials of the New Mexico State Land Office, and for the purpose of protecting the treasure and personal property which they had underground, closed and locked the shaft. Since that time the shaft has, of course, been broken into.

"I cannot avoid adding at this point that we were simply astounded to learn that Col. Jaffe had not made any attempt whatsoever to examine or search the Noss title. I must say, further, that our search on the title discloses that no one has ever before attacked the Noss title. The workings on Victoria Peak have always been designated as the Noss claims. The fact is that Col. Jaffe is the only one who has ever questioned their title or their right to any treasure located on the property.

"One further comment on Lt. Col. Jaffe's announced position: The military has no right to attack the title of the Nosses to either treasure or minerals; the military has no right to remove and sell minerals or treasure trove, and it is not a title-issuing authority which can question the title of a citizen, especially to personal property. We think it is important to note a legal distinction here: This is not alone the usual claim by citizens to the right to co-use of the surface with the government in order to mine minerals. This is a claim by citizens of the right to enter the reservation and remove personal property which they contend, under the rules relating to the discovery and possession of treasure, belongs to them. The exercise of their right to remove their personal property is especially made necessary in order to protect it from operations of the character conducted on the site which gave rise to this situation."

In closing: "Incidentally, your curiosity may be aroused, as mine has been, by the fact that the treasure, if it exists, has, according to the sworn inventory furnished me, a value in the order of one-half billion dollars, with an exposed gold ore body worth many times that amount. There is good evidence too, that the caves contain records and objects of art which could produce a wealth of information on the cultural and religious history of the southwest."

In his reply the General again repeated, somewhat more elaborately, the Army's position. It would exclude "all persons from the Range who were not directly engaged in the conduct of the missile test programs carried on at White Sands Missile Range . . . . the area to which you seek access has been subject to posting and police surveillance . . . . and all trespassers found there have been apprehended, evicted, and prosecuted." He explained that the operations in mid-1961 were carried on in the area "pursuant to joint instructions of the departments of the Treasury and the Army . . . . . . That action was designed solely to bring to an end rumors concerning the impalpable existence of some treasure trove at White Sands Missile Range which, the Treasury department advises, have been exploited to the prejudice of numerous persons since 1939 and whose existence . . . . . has been a source of harassment to this Command and to the Treasury department."

Then the letter aimed a jab at Doc Noss:

"In this connection, the Acting Director of the Mint wrote to the Secretary of the Army:

Our files show that back in the thirties there was a doctor who duped many people on a gold hoard scheme from an operation near the location of this so-called hoard. Since the thirties, we have had hundreds of inquiries concerning a large hoard of gold in this area. I am of the opinion that the doctor, in his efforts to defraud, may have stored some non-

gold bars in a cave so that he could show his prospective buyers the so-called gold cache.

I am interested in your granting permission to enter the cave because I should like to put an end to this rumor. I have not gone into the question of ownership as I am positive the bars will not contain gold.

"The effort (requested by Fiege and Gasiewicz) made pursuant to the mentioned joint directive was not and will not be completed. Nor did it result in the revelation of any gold or indeed anything of value."

Martin wrote on December 11:

Dear General Shinkle:

I was out of the city on Friday and Saturday of last week, but found your letter of December 6 on my desk this morning. While we appreciate the frank statement of your position and the courteous tone of your letter, you will recognize, however, that it does not solve the question presented to us by the fact that according to what appear to be authoritative reports, a quantity of gold bars was discovered and some of them, at least, removed from the premises a couple of years ago by military personnel and this problem is further complicated by the fact that we are still at a loss to understand why responsible officers of your command found it necessary to deny the existence of operations on the property which were very certainly taking place.

In light of these circumstances I feel that unless our clients direct otherwise, we will have to continue our investigation which ultimately, I suppose, can only be implemented by the commencement of actions against those who have tampered with the Noss property, in the course of which they can be required to give testimony under oath concerning their activities and the findings, if any.

In view of your assurance that the recent operations have not and will not be completed, I do not feel that there is any further need for emergency action to protect the interest of our clients and in reliance upon those assurances, we will proceed in a more deliberate and orderly fashion. In that connection, it has occurred to me that if we could be given access to files or records containing the reports of Colonel Gasiewicz and the two alleged discoverers of the quantity of gold bars, including, perhaps, the results of the polygraph test and the records, if any, concerning the ultimate disposition of the bar or bars recovered, our problem might be greatly simplified. At the same time, it might be helpful for us to see whatever information or reports might be available to support the apparent view of the Treasury department that this entire affair is a hoax (complete with pseudo gold bars) perpetrated by Dr. Noss.

If there is any basis for us to cooperate along the line of the inspection of records I have just suggested, we would appreciate hearing from you.

In the meantime, please be assured of our continuing desire to interfere as little as possible with the regular military work of the White Sands Missile Range.

With kind regards.

Very truly yours,
COLLINS, HUGHES, MARTIN, PRINGLE & SCHELL
By Robert Martin

General Shinkle had some afterthoughts. He informed us in a subsequent letter that Colonel Gasiewicz was never a member of his command, that he is an Air Force officer at Holloman Air Force Base and that he had none of the records that made reference to Gasiewicz's activity in connection with the gold bars.

He further said the individuals who claimed to have made the discovery included two present and two former members of the Air Force and not the Army, "who at all times acted in their private capacities, and that since this matter was brought up these men have been put under official surveillance for the purpose of ensuring that, if anything were present at or removed from the site, it would be safeguarded and turned over immediately to the Treasury department for disposition according to law."

General Shinkle's plan to exclude all persons "absolutely" and, "to limit work in the area strictly to missile test programs," was communicated personally by him through a telephone conversation to E. S. Johnny Walker, State Commissioner of Lands, at Santa Fe. Walker replied he saw nothing wrong with the plan, that he himself was trying to stay away from the matter, adding, "the Noss attorneys will probably raise hell, judging from the fact that they have filed an inventory setting out in detail the objects to be found." A memo of that conversation was prepared by Oscar Jordan and made a part of Land Office files open to the public.

An Associated Press story (May 25, 1962) drew excited reactions from a number of Noss claimants, no less so than Ova Noss who had read it in her Clovis paper and succeeded in reaching me after midnight, insisting that contact be made immediately and the government be advised that the gold bars had come from the Noss caverns.

The story read:

ARREST ARIZONANS
FOR HOARDING GOLD

ILLEGAL POSSESSION OF 2½ BARS
OF BULLION IS FEDERAL CHARGE

New York, May 24. (AP)-The government today held two Arizona men on charges of illegally possessing gold from a Western mine at a time when the nation is concerned about its gold balance.

The men, Stanley Lane, 46, and Joseph Valle, 39, both of Phoenix were placed under $10,000 bond each on charges of possessing two and a half bars of bullion valued at $8,000.

Federal authorities said they were members of a ring that had "unlimited access" to the mine, which was unidentified.

"The government regards this as a most serious offense, particularly in view of the very serious situation this country faces regarding the gold situation," said Grenville Garside, assistant U. S. attorney.

Lane and Valle waived a hearing before Earl N. Bishop, U.S. commissioner, pending possible grand jury action.

Garside said Secret Service agents and police arrested the men late yesterday in a New York apartment belonging to a sister of Lane. The bullion, Garside said, was found in Lane's suitcase.

To Fiege in person

Was *rigor mortis* setting in on the Noss mystery? The meeting with Shinkle hardly deepened our faith in the likelihood of a re-entry and we faced the question of whether it was sensible to devote the time and effort required to attack the wall of bureaucratic indifference.

In the midst of these meditations, Martin called to advise his trial schedule had suffered as a result of his Noss activities and expressed the hope I would pursue the case alone. Whereupon I called upon George O'Laughlin, an experienced trial attorney in Kansas City, who had shown a continuing interest in the treasure trove case. Upon a review of its status at that point, we both agreed the next logical move was to ascertain the whereabouts of Captain Leonard Fiege and, if possible, arrange a visit. The first chore proved easy; the Air Force advised Fiege was stationed at Holloman in Alamogordo, N.M.

We decided to pay the captain a surprise visit.

We appeared at the Fiege home at Holloman on April 30, 1962, shortly after lunch time.

Mrs. Fiege, young, very pretty, admitted us and shortly the captain entered the living room. His smile vanished quickly when we explained our mission. It was soon evident both were emotional about the treasure trove; Fiege said there was nothing he wished to discuss. We assured him we were not certain all the Noss claims were valid and hoped he might help clarify the matter.

He was immediately critical of the Noss family. As he warmed to the subject, face flushed, he went deeper into details.

111

He said he had, in 1959, entered a fault at Victoria Peak and after some difficulty came upon a room which, in his words, "contained something," "I'm not going to say what it was, lead, copper, silver or gold."

He described his descent into the shaft as dangerous and at one point had difficulty squeezing through a narrow aperture.

He said he returned to the surface and asked one of his companions, Berlett, to go down into the fault. Berlett, smallest of the group, agreed but nothing was removed from the room.

He refused to specify what he saw in the cavern, nor how many other rooms were there.

"I am not going to tell you what is down there or whether it has value."

Before leaving the peak area he said he blocked the entrance with boulders and earth to prevent "someone else discovering the cave." But in doing so had caused an excess of earth and rock to fall into the crevice, and men and equipment probably would be needed to get back in.

He gave details of several steps he took later to get official permission to return and remove what he had discovered. He said he went to the office of Colonel Gasiewicz at the Air Force base a few days later and asked whether a person was entitled to keep something of value found on a military base. Gasiewicz told him that would depend upon the circumstances. Finally, he said, two years later he did obtain permission, "through high official sources in spite of the opposition of both General Shinkle and Colonel Jaffe" at the missile range. He said he was given "a guard of a hundred men" at the scene of the mining operations "and we would have had the stuff out of there in two weeks if Mrs. Noss hadn't interfered."

The reference to Mrs. Noss' "interference" was to the spying by the four friends of the Noss family who had observed military personnel operations at Victoria Peak. If that hadn't happened, he said, he was prepared to turn his discovery over to a court for a ruling on the true owners.

He then accused the Nosses of telling different, conflicting stories. He said he checked documents in Washington and found support for his position. Further, he had gone over records which prove "Doc" Noss was guilty of foisting a bunco on a number of people — "I don't know whether he got lead bars and put them in a cave or not."

He brushed aside the possibility of a valid claim by Mrs. Noss. "I don't have any sympathy for her at all."

His comments about General Shinkle were almost as harsh.

He would not specifically say who had given him the men and equipment to conduct the 1961 excavation but "it wasn't Shinkle." He said he had gone to Washington and the permission had come, as he put it, "from the top down".

He had given the matter much time and thought in the three years since his discovery, and had taken his plane over Victoria Peak almost daily for a considerable period to observe whether anyone was trying to get into the caverns.

Shortly before our departure, Mrs. Fiege whispered something to her husband. He went to the phone with the comment he was going to call his lawyer who, it developed, was a Maj. Bruce Eisen, also stationed at the base.

We became immediately aware that Major Eisen was not happy that Fiege was talking to us. At one point Fiege exclaimed, "I'm not letting them box me in!" Before the telephone conversation ended, I had suggested that Eisen might wish to meet with us but Fiege shook his head. He said his attorney had nothing to say to us. He had a claim to what he had found, insisting that his discovery was in no way related to the Noss treasure. He repeated there was no such treasure and again described Doc Noss as a fraud.

Reviewing the contents of the visit, it appeared the most significant was Fiege's exclamation that he would have removed all the gold if Mrs. Noss had not interfered. That admission led us to speculate further. Captain Fiege swore he did not remove a single bar from several stacks numbering perhaps a hundred or more. He accompanied the official excavation expedition to the spot of the discovery; no gold was found. What happened to it? Was it spirited away by another finder with or without Fiege's knowledge? Did Fiege exercise what he saw as his right as a true finder (and there is legal basis for that presumption) and had carted it away with the help of, and in association with, certain fellow officers?

We thought some light might be shed on the Fiege claim by a check of Secret Service records pertaining to lie detector tests. In late November, George O'Laughlin and I met with John P. Jones, the Secret Service agent in charge of the Denver office. By coincidence Oscar Jordan, the attorney for the State Land Office, was also there. He quickly explained the primary interest of the Land Office was to prevent any claimant to the treasure trove receiving preferential treatment over any other.

We outlined in some detail the basic contentions of the Noss family and explained why we felt the Noss claims were entitled to priority.

Jones brought out a file folder containing a dozen sheets of typewriter paper stapled together, statements made by Fiege and Berlett, and read a few paragraphs. He referred to a development with which we were familiar, Colonel Gasiewicz's call to Oscar Jordan to advise the Air Force personnel had found a bar of gold and Jordan's advice to turn the bar over to federal authorities.

In the statements to the Secret Service, Fiege and Berlett said they had partly excavated the shaft and had come across approximately 100 bars of gold bullion, that they had climbed back out of the shaft and pushed in rocks and debris to seal off the opening, then consulted with Gasiewicz. The statement said they did not take away any of the bars and that both were present during the Army's unsuccessful effort to retrieve the gold.

We asked about the lie-detector tests given Fiege. Jones replied that the test results indicated Fiege was telling the truth when he said he had found gold bars.

In late December Bradley and Gray, two of the four who had spied on the military working atop Victoria Peak, again visited the area, reported to Ova that they saw a helicopter, probably a security measure, hovering above the peak. At one point they were certain their presence was detected but managed to leave without difficulty. It was a close enough call to persuade them to make it their last spy mission.

Still, both men were to remain active in Ova's behalf, later succeeding in persuading U. S. Rep. George Mahon of Texas to write to the Secretary of the Army asking for a review of the matter. The reply (from General H. A. Gerhardt): "The Army has no interest in determining either the existence or ownership of any gold . . . it is the Army's intention to deny access to all persons . . . until the United States' requirements for the Missile Range may no longer exist."

Next, E. S. Johnny Walker, New Mexico Commissioner of Public Lands, made a similar request to General Shinkle at White Sands but Shinkle was adamant. His policy of exclusion, he wrote to Walker late in April, was in the best interests of the United States, asserting that "to take any action at this time along such lines as you suggest would only serve to lend credence to otherwise impalpable allegations."

At this point we could not have even guessed that

before the year was out the Army would swallow its own official words. What was to lead to at least a temporary reversal of Army attitude was totally unexpected — an avid interest in treasure troves on the part of a man named Loren E. (Les) Smith, an official of the Gaddis Mining Company of Denver.

Smith had researched the treasure trove records for many months and was satisfied Noss' discovery was highly credible. He felt the involvement of other persons was too extensive to brush the story aside as just another gold fable of the Southwest.

After several weeks of negotiations, the Gaddis company agreed to give Ova Noss an immediate payment of $800 and $800 every month until such time as the treasures are reduced to possession or the overall project abandoned. Further, the company would bear all expenses of obtaining permits and conducting re-entry operations at the peak. It agreed to spend, if necessary, between $200,000 and $250,000 in the effort to reach the treasure rooms.

In return, Ova assigned the company 40 percent of her interest in the treasures. If for any reason the company failed to reach the caverns, the 40 percent would revert to her.

In this period, my associate George O'Laughlin and I drafted the petition for a lawsuit by Mrs. Noss challenging the Defense Department's right to keep her from re-entering the Missile Range and removing certain personal properties. The Gaddis company fully supported our decision to resort to litigation and engaged an attorney to assist us, Victor C. Green of Rowley, Breen & Bowen, Tucumcari, N. M.

Circumstances, however, soon developed that would cause us to withdraw the action.

In early June, 1962, newspaper stories announced the transfer of Maj. Gen. John G. Shinkle from the Missile Range to duty in Paris, France, with the U. S. Army element of the North Atlantic Treaty Organization

International Staff.

He was replaced at White Sands by Brig. Gen. John Frederick Thorlin.

Without delay, we contacted the new commandant's office for an appointment. It was refused but he agreed to visit with us by phone.

The drift of our conversation with Thorlin was not unexpected. He asked for our understanding of his need for time in order to acquaint himself with his new duties. While he had heard "bits and pieces" about the Noss treasure matter he said there was a wide gap in his knowledge of it. Until he could acquaint himself with the details, a matter requiring a few months, he was compelled to enforce his predecessor's ban against any entry or exploration at the peak.

In mid-March the Securities and Exchange Commission in Washington, taking note of the fraud possibilities arising from publicity about the treasure trove, alerted all field agents to watch for attempted sales of any interests, stock or contractual rights in any exploration activities or in companies proposing to explore for or recover the Victoria Peak treasure. This prompted us to send word to Ova Noss and Harold Beckwith, cautioning them to refrain for the time being from selling or even discussing sale of interests in the treasure. The Gaddis arrangement, we felt, was not affected; that was an arm's-length understanding between parties fully aware of the high risks involved.

Memorandum to the file:

10:30 a.m., April 9, 1962: A Mr. F. W. Jung (pronounced *Young*) of 7633 Washington in Kansas City telephoned to say he had read the account of the Noss mine in The Star, had just received a letter from an associate of his in Alamogordo named Richard Wm. Cole, the letter stating that in 1956 an Ernest R. Raehrs (pronounced *Rares*) went down 180 feet into the mineshaft. He knew Doc Noss. He would very much like to pass some of his information on to you.

117

The Gaddis sortie

Loren E. (Les) Smith, an engineer of skill and experience, had checked into virtually every facet of the Noss story. With the firm's president, William H. Gaddis, as a frequent passenger, a private plane took them thousands of miles in the effort to track down clues and interview persons even remotely connected with the history of the case. To support their conviction that a treasure existed in Victoria Peak, they put $250,000 earnest money in escrow, all or any necessary part of it to be used in the attempt to reach the caverns, once government permission was obtained. Smith made a technical study of the Victoria Peak area and environs, then reduced the findings to report form.

He met with General Thorlin at White Sands in mid-September and a month later submitted to the Army a 15-page exploration program, including maps and aerial photos of the Victoria Peak area. The company had sent the first of the $800 monthly payments to Ova, even though at that time it had no idea when or if it would receive government approval to enter the Range.

A familiar problem erupted early in the talks with Thorlin: the Defense department's concern over setting a precedent; permitting a single claimant onto the Missile Range would open the door to a multiplicity of similar requests. So, the Gaddis effort appeared fore-doomed.

Then a surprising turn in the situation occurred: an ingenious plan was suggested by Les Smith. He proposed that the Museum of New Mexico make application for the permit to explore the peak, citing as justification the Museum's interest in the heirloom treasures and artifacts in the caverns, objects certain to contribute greatly to the cultural and social history of New Mexico. More importantly, it would solve the treasure-trove mystery and put to rest the endless rumors and complications. Whatever was found in the way of gold and treasures would be placed with the appropriate court of law to determine the rightful owners.

The Smith proposal was quickly endorsed by both the Museum and Land Office. It took a little longer to bring the Defense department and the Army into line but they finally agreed to go along, encouraged by strong recommendations from two congressmen, Mahon of Texas and Morris of New Mexico.

Then, unexpectedly, someone put the squeeze on Ova Noss. She was persuaded to sign a waiver which cancelled whatever rights she had to sue the Army or the White Sands Missile Range Command.

It was an extraordinary move and one which Ova should have called to the attention of her attorneys. Without our knowledge she signed the document at the request of Gaddis Company officials. The waiver document, consisting of only three pages, stipulated that in order "to induce the Army to give its consent and approval to the Museum's application . . . . . and to permit the removal of all treasure or personal property claimed by Mrs. Noss . . . . . Mrs. Noss formally and expressly waives all rights, claims or demands which she may or could have against the United States or the Secretary of Defense, *by reason of its alleged unlawful taking and withholding of her personal property,* and agrees to forebear any suit or action against the United States for recovery of such property."

Ova sent me a signed copy of the document, whereupon I immediately wrote to her:

March 8, 1963

Dear Ova:

I sincerely wish you had let us see the Waiver Agreement before you signed it.

By signing it you have waived your right to sue the government or its agents even though it should develop that the government or its agents had spirited off your gold. That is, you cannot bring such a suit until the government's work is completed and it abandons the Missile Range. Not likely to happen in our lifetime.

You have waived YOUR right to sue; we have not as interest holders. I am sorry you signed. It will not be an important surrender, however, unless it is determined that someone on the base did in fact steal your treasure.

Why would the Army insist on such a waiver? It was an indirect admission that there had been an unauthorized intrusion into the Noss cavern by military personnel; so it was deemed necessary to eliminate Ova's right to resort to litigation to recapture the gold bars. Ova's signature on the document placed the Army beyond the reach of judicial action.

A defense department license was issued to the Museum on July 11, 1963, for a 30-day exploration period. Thereupon the Museum subcontracted the work to the Gaddis Mining Company. The agreement required Gaddis to pay all expenses of the project, including per-diem wages of Museum personnel assigned to the task and the cost of Army security guards.

Victoria Peak itself rises approximately 400 feet from the Hembrillo basin floor. An adjoining ridge south of the peak is about 300 feet above the basin floor. Victoria's elevation is 5,525 feet and the basin rim 6,000 feet. Water was available for domestic and drilling purposes at a spring near the base of the peak.

The exploration area mapped out by the Gaddis company was limited to the triangular piece of land formed by three principal arroyos flanking Victoria Peak. The license did not permit a search for possible clues outside this tract. No photographs were allowed and special permission had to be given for underground photos, if any were needed.

In a period of less than 12 hours the Gaddis company moved a considerable number of pieces of heavy equipment onto the site, including a bulldozer, drill rigs, compressors, recorder and "shooting" trucks.

Loren E. Smith was placed in charge of the work. His Museum contacts were Dr. Fred Wendorf and Dr. Alfred E. Dittert, Jr., both of the Museum's Division of Anthropology, and Chester Johnson, staff anthropologist at the site. Wendorf would help direct operations.

It was not in the plan to excavate Doc Noss' old, collapsed shaft. The shaft would be by-passed and instead a new access would be attempted by drilling horizontally into a point some 200 feet below the top of the peak, thus hopefully to reach the old tunnel leading to the treasure rooms. It was estimated that the new approach would have to be several hundred feet long in order to penetrate the tunnel.

The entire program was expected to be completed in twenty-one days, work proceeding on a continuous 7-day-week basis. The time would be reduced if the estimated drilling depth was overstated and the rock encountered was soft. The twenty-one days would include 7 days for the seismic survey, 10 days for the drilling program and 4 days to complete the access shaft.

The work began on July 19, 1963, with workmen assigned to all three tasks simultaneously — archaeological, seismic and gravity surveys. A Laboratory of Anthropology site number LA 2527 was given to the area.

The seismic survey consisted of setting five geophones, or recording devices, at regular intervals, setting off explosives and recording the time of delay incident to the passing of the shock waves through the rocks. The purpose was to locate cavities (caves) in the rocks by recording any delays larger than normal. Although anomalies or unexplained delays were located, no cavities were found at these points.

The gravity survey consisted of measuring the density of the rocks by the pull of gravity on the gravity meter, and noting the change in density from point to point. Any reversal in trend, up or down, indicated an anomaly that should be investigated.

Although the gravity survey was more reliable than the seismic, no caverns were located. In several places, large rubble-filled cracks were found but not considered meaningful. About 80 holes were drilled during the course of the project. The last penetration was into one of the previously explored passages, the so-called Soldiers' Hole, in which gold bars reportedly were found.

At the expiration of the 30-day permit the Museum asked for more time. An additional and final thirty days was granted. The Gaddis people now decided to drill another tunnel, starting at a predetermined point in the direction of Soldiers' Hole. Again Doc Noss' old shaft was rejected; the probing and digging in the 24 years since its closing had drastically changed its features. Also, to open the old passage would require timbering and removal of considerble rubble, tasks which would take longer than the period of the extension.

In the second try, a tunnel was driven 218 feet into the side of the peak, and was believed to have intersected the "Soldiers' Hole", possibly quite near the caved shaft. There were tense moments as caved rocks were removed, but only undisturbed water-deposited silt lay in the crevice. The area in which gold bars were said to have been found was not reached. The stone and silt wall came into view two days before the end of the extension period, at which point the project was halted. On September 7, 1963, the Gaddis company left the scene.

The $200,000 mission was a failure, the mystery of Victoria Peak unruffled, still contemptuous of its pursuers.

A note of frustration ran through the Museum's summary of the Gaddis probe. It said the exploration had uncovered nothing except eleven shards dating back to the 14th century, adding, "An incredible amount of labor has been expended on the hill."

The Museum further stated:

"It was the purpose of this project to prove or disprove the claim of Doc Noss that Victoria Peak is the site of the mine worked by Padre La Rue. It is the concensus of the project personnel, judging from the surface rocks, that this peak cannot be the location of the mine of La Rue. The more than 1,000 feet of sedimentary beds, composed of Pennsylvania, Mississipian and earlier eras, is cut in Victoria Peak by a fine-grained, diabasic, diorite dike, containing no definable segregations of metallic minerals, but having a high iron content. There are no tailings or slag dumps on the peak and none is visible on the nearby hills. Any such should be obvious if they existed, as only 150 years have passed.

"The above leads to the conclusion that if a treasure was or is here, it was brought from some other location and stored here by persons as yet unknown. The two months' exploration produced no evidence indicating the location of the treasure or its origin ...... The conflicting stories of the persons who say they have worked with the Nosses and have knowledge of the treasure have only made a confused situation more confusing."

Confused or not, skeptical or not, the Museum report did little to alter the belief of many persons that Doc Noss had come upon a fabulous treasure. Their faith was to be strengthened by events to come.

In the course of extensive preparations for the operations at the peak, the Gaddis company had failed to keep us informed of progress in its negotiations with the Museum and the Army. Keeping counsel apace with developments was a matter of professional courtesy. We had assumed there would be a "no comment" response to all press inquiries, but the growing breach in our relationship did not deter Gaddis representatives; they conducted talks with our client, often without our knowledge or consent. Still, our feelings were held in check in view of the importance of the overall objective.

I wrote Les Smith in early April:

"I talked with Mrs. Noss a few moments ago and she imparts the good news that you are about to obtain a permit of entry and plan to move your equipment onto the site in about two weeks.

"If so, this is a major step, and I am sure you are making provision for George O'Laughlin and me to be a part of the official group at the site. I have made two efforts to reach you by phone in recent weeks.

We stand ready, of course, to move at a moment's notice, and trust you will keep us directly advised as to developments.

For 30 days work went on at the peak and still no word from Les Smith. Nonetheless I went about the task of obtaining a temporary permit to allow me an hour or two visit at the scene of the digging. More telephone calls and letters to Smith went unanswered. I learned he was spending most of the nights in a trailer home at the foot of the peak, occasionally retreating to a hotel room in Las Cruces for a shower and routine chores connected with the exploration.

If puzzled by the Gaddis company's indifference to our

position as counsel for the Nosses, we were increasingly distressed by the scornful attitude toward my efforts to obtain a permit. From August 21, for a period of almost two weeks, I encountered a bureaucratic maze of unkept promises and assurances from Museum officials.

In the course of the frustrating experience I kept day-to-day notes:

Aug. 24: Switchboard operator at Las Cruces motel confirmed Smith had received word of my telephone call of yesterday, that it had been "radioed" to him at his trailer at the site. She said he said he would call. How she got that info was not made clear, having said earlier he had not returned to motel.

Aug. 24: Received call at my Colorado Springs motel room from Col. Marmon of White Sands advising Gen. Thorlin would be at the base only on Monday next and would be happy to see me then . . . Advised I should get clearance to visit peak from the Museum of N.M., Div. of Anthropology, via Dr. Fred Wendorf, Santa Fe; that the Army could not permit anyone at Noss site without some "routine" approval from Wendorff; that the Div. of Anthro. was in charge of the operation. I asked Col. Marmon's cooperation in so advising Les Smith to contact Wendorf and obtain such clearance for me. Col. Marmon said it would be easy for him. Before the day was out he would get the word out to Smith at the site.

Aug. 24: Called O'Laughlin (K.C.) to inform him of refusal of Smith to return my calls. Directed George to write a letter (on law firm stationery) to Dr. Fred Wendorf at Santa Fe, outlining our interest in Noss case, and advising Wendorf that I would be in Santa Fe Monday or Tuesday. I agreed Gaddis Mining

Co.'s behavior arbitrary in keeping from us for 30 days the word of the inception of digging operations at the Missile Range.

Aug. 25: Telephoned Robt. Martin, (assoc. counsel) at his home to advise him substantially of the same points communicated to G. T. O'Laughlin. (Still no word from Smith at Las Cruces.) Advised I was holding here in Colo. Spgs. over weekend on possibility conference with Gaddis and Smith would develop, either here or in Denver.

Aug. 25: Drafted letter to Brig. Gen. Thorlin at White Sands advising him of my movements and expressing regrets that I would not be able to keep my appointment with him, on the 26th, because of the necessity of securing letter from Dr. Wendorf.

Dictated following letter to secretary over phone, to be mailed to Smith:
Les:
   I had a long talk today with Bill Gaddis. Please contact me by phone at the La Posada (Santa Fe) the afternoon of the 27th or anytime in the following three or four days. I'd like very much to visit with you even though I recognize the impossibility of my becoming an official observer at the scene of the exploration. However, I am hopeful you will possess the magic to let me hold forth there at least for an hour or two inasmuch as this is an occasion we've all been dreaming about for many, many years. Good luck!

Aug. 27: Conferred with Oscar Jordan, New Mexico Land Office Atty. Advised letter of confirmation for access to the Noss site at Missile Range must be signed by Dr. Alfred E. Dittert, Jr., Curator,

Museum of New Mexico. Went to Museum offices and obtained letter of confirmation.

Aug. 27: Called Col. Marmon and arranged for visit to Noss site. Colonel agreeably offered jeep transportation to the site. Trip would take 2-3 hours.

Aug. 28: Complications re my transportation from base headquarters to Victoria Peak. Talked twice to Col. Marmon, and once to Col. Wade, who made it appear inadvisable to attempt to reach the peak by private vehicle.

Col. Marmon transmitted my message to Les Smith who reportedly agreed to call me tonight. Strongly suggest to Col. Wade that this turnabout on the part of the Army was most distressing. Smith did not call.

Aug. 28: Army (via Provost Marshall Wade) agrees to escort me to guard point within 2 miles of exploration site. At guard point, I could be admitted only by field representative of Museum of N.M.

Aug. 29: Departed Las Cruces by Army jeep at 9 a.m. Reached guard point after harrowing 3-hour trip through trackless and treacherous mountainous terrain in Hembrillo Basin, over a road which natives call "Journey of Death." My desire to continue to site now much abated. Fear jeep easily overturned by deep ruts. Physically exhausting. Driver (a Pvt.) appeared to enjoy trip.

Aug. 30: 11:40 a.m. Waiting at guard point. Museum representative Chester Johnson refuses to acknowledge letter of admission signed by Dr. Dittert, stating Dittert had revoked letter. I strongly urged validity of letter and my reliance upon it; otherwise

I would not have made trip to the area. Three hours of dispute and radio-relayed conversation with Dittert. Dittert confers with Dr. Wendorf at the Museum, who says, "It made no difference to the Museum whether visitor is given entry." Whereupon Johnson agreed, having been advised in the meantime by me that his negative position was an excessive exercise of authority and most assuredly would result in court action against him personally.

2 p.m.: I was then escorted to the scene of the digging. Men working in new tunnel. Not visible to outside observer. Few large pieces of equipment. Activity not all that great. Advised Les Smith was not at the site of the exploration, checked out at 9:20 p.m. previous night. Apparent he had made no effort to assist me in my efforts and refused to return my calls.

3 p.m.: Left area, returned to Las Cruces.

The following day, as I prepared to leave the Las Cruces motel to return to K.C., Les Smith appeared. He said he was staying at a hotel only 2 blocks away, admitted he knew of my efforts to reach him. I advised him that, apart from obvious discourtesies, the Gaddis Company was engaging in legal activity that in our view exceeds their "agency" arrangement with the Nosses. He proceeded to recite details of numerous difficulties faced in the present exploration endeavor. Then he revealed developments, which, if proven to be true, were startling in the extreme. From these disclosures, it was evident Gaddis representatives were negotiating with persons whose rights to the treasure trove (in the Gaddis Co.'s oppinion) are superior to those of the Noss family.

"I want to remind you," Smith said, "that the operations at the peak are the result of a contract between Gaddis and the Museum."

"What you're saying is that you may carry on talks that are independent of your agreement with the Noss family."

"Exactly."

I asked him what he felt would be the effect of such activity upon the agreement with the Nosses by which his Gaddis company received 40 percent of Ova Noss' interest in the treasures.

I need not have asked the question. Obviously, the Gaddis company was operating on two fronts, using one as a hedge against the other. Smith did not elaborate further on how far negotiations had gone with second parties.

His next comment was totally out of character for the tight-lipped Les Smith. He said he was convinced beyond doubt that within the week or 10 days at the latest they would reach a cache of gold bullion (1,400 bars) of estimated value of $42 million. He indicated the Gaddis Co. may contend the "find" is not part of the so-called Noss treasure.

As a matter of fact, he said, Mrs. Noss' own story of the discovery eliminates her claim to the gold which his company is seeking. He further stated that the caverns initially were entered by Doc Noss and another man named (euphonically) Seraphine together and that the two jointly found the caverns. Smith says he is in contact with the former Mrs. Seraphine — "she is in the area and we are trying to locate Seraphine himself."

Letter to Robert Martin   June 16, 1964
Dear Bob,

Earlier this month while in Santa Fe I chanced a telephone call to Les Smith, who, describing my call as timely, proceeds to disclose for the first time that the Gaddis company and an unnamed Texas mining company had joined hands to undertake a second effort to find and enter the Noss caverns at the Missile Range. He said permission would be given "as a result of contacts on the highest Washington levels."

He said the Texas outfit has been given a percentage of the Gaddis share of the trove, and in return for said interest the Texas people would advance the cash necessary for the second exploration.

I have since had opportunity to reflect on this business of interests which, it seems, Mrs. Noss has been selling with orgiastic glee in the past two decades. This much seems supportable: Our 5% was given us by Mrs. Noss BEFORE the Gaddis people received their 40%. What we have, actually, is 5% of what Mrs. Noss owned at the time of our contact with her.

So the question of what she owns at this point may be quite decisive, if I may commit myself to a rugged understatement.

As to our interest in the trove, the algebraic formula reads thusly: Mrs. Noss' current interest less 5% less 40%.

Now, if Mrs. Noss' interest was zero at the time of the 5% transfer to us, we may be said to own 5% of nothing.

Gaddis may be said to have 40% of nothing, less 5% of nothing, or 40% of zero less 5%.

The Texas people have one-half of the Gaddis interest, or 50% of nothing.

Thus is the fate of all treasure trovers.

By the way, these calculations may be enormously significant in late August, when (Les says) they hope to be back on Victoria Peak.

Pack up!

PAK

Nothing short of a miracle could get the Gaddis people past the roadblocks to yet another exploration at Victoria Peak. They had had their day in court and the results, though inconclusive, only served to firm up the attitude of Army brass. Their judgment was concise and seemingly beyond appeal: No gold was found; therefore no more exploration at Victoria Peak.

So, not unexpectedly, silence settles over the treasure trove. Almost as deep and impenetrable as the mine shaft itself. But lost-treasure hunting is an act of faith. The spirit of the true believer is not ruffled by temporary adversities, for he knows the failure is not in the treasure trove but in the hunter himself.

Ova's faith was not even slightly ruffled. "Doc" had found a fabulous treasure and gophered some of it out of the rugged earth and hid it in tunnels and drifts that honeycomb the hills. Oh, yes, she knew how such things went. When gold is found and actually got in hand, the story of the discovery gets out, but never the story of what actually happens to the gold. She could not put aside her thoughts about the military. The vision clung like a bad dream, recurring time and again with tantalizing vividness. The military had found gold bars, no doubt a cache which Doc had stashed in some hole, then later attested to their find in a signed affidavit. Then two years went by; they said they were returning to the hiding place to possess the gold. After two years! Is one expected to believe so golden a discovery was permitted to remain, unguarded and unpossessed, in some earthen grave for so long a time, subject to the winds, rains and caprice of fate? That was not the way people would act, in uniform or out.

Nor did she for a moment believe the military had come upon the bulk of the treasure held captive in the bowels of Victoria Peak; but even of that she could not be completely certain, for there remained the nagging possibility that having stripped clean one little hiding place, they may have wandered into the strange, dark drift and thence into the caverns that held the fabled treasure. She doubted that most earnestly; such a discovery would indeed be most difficult to conceal for any period of time. But the cache itself, that was a discovery openly declared and admitted upon oath, and knowledge of the circumstances kept within the neat, cozy confines of military comradeship. Then the most telling disclosure of all: A corporation formed by military and ex-military personnel "to protect what we have found."

Little wonder Ova Noss was deeply resentful; faced time and again with terse military pronouncements that no treasure exists or ever existed at Victoria Peak, and the whole business branded a sham and a fraud.

The Noss family continued to forage about in the bureaucratic jungle, voicing the same dull entreaty — "Let us back on the hill." A pilgrimage here and a crusade there, and always with the same result: cold rejection by the military. The attitude of the White Sands Command seemed as unchangeable as it was inexplicable.

In this period Howard Bryan of the Albuquerque Tribune kept in close touch. He was preparing a series of lengthy articles about the gold story — ten install-ments over a period of several weeks. He had evidenced an open mind throughout, and reflected that attitude in his stories. Privately on several occasions he expressed disappointment and surprise over the summary rejection by White Sands.

I wrote Bryan on January 15, 1974:

I am sorry I have put you to some bother about the FBI report on M. E. Noss. An old friend, Clarence Kelley, now FBI chief, has indicated there is a specific way to request such a report.

To the point of this letter: I am deeply upset by the off-hand attitude of agents of the U. S.

Department of the Army toward Mrs. Noss. We have patiently met every demand of the department with respect to her request to be permitted to enter the Missile Range so she may recapture what she says is her personal property. She asks only a few hours to seek out a hiding place where, she is confident, there is a cache of gold bars hidden by her late husband.

The evident attitude of the Department of the Army is one normally reserved for idiots and fools. The servants in Washington have turned arrogant masters. Gently, whimsically, and hopefully, we put them into office, pay for their room and board, then see ourselves become pawns in a tragic game of democratic hocus-pocus.

The latest response from the office of the Assistant Secretary of the Department of the Army is a bland, open-faced insult to Mrs. Noss, a display of caprice hidden under a veneer of mock sobriety. I say to hell with any service that trods upon those it is pledged to serve. It was proper for the Army to send its own agents upon the Noss site, secretly and clandestinely, but it is wrong to permit Mrs. Noss to do so. The objections being urged against her request simply were not effective when the Army moved in upon her diggings. In doing so, the Army violated an agreement between the state of New Mexico and the U. S. Government.

The $25,000 windfall

The unusual events of 1973 began on what Ova Noss viewed as a proper note — a money offer from a syndicate in Salt Lake City. The amount was such that I cautioned her to keep enthusiasm in rein, at least until we learned what the parties wanted in return for their offer — a total of $150,000 of which they would pay $25,000 immediately and the balance at $5,000 a month. Their demand: 51% of Ova's interest in the treasure trove, giving effective control over whatever rights Ova possessed at the time.

I was not able to learn much about the group making the offer. All identities were cloaked in secrecy. The contact was a young attorney of a reputable Salt Lake City law firm. A contract was drafted following several conversations and a single meeting in Clovis. We advised that Ova would surrender 49%, not 51%, and ultimately that division was agreed upon.

In order to avoid any appearance of fraud, the contract stipulated that the syndicate would receive 49% of whatever interest it is ultimately determined Mrs. Noss possessed at the time.

Only one name was mentioned in the course of our discussions, John Walton, who somehow eluded all our efforts to reach him. Then one day I received a call from a man who identified himself as John Walton. He assured us he was a member of the syndicate and we discussed various aspects of the impending deal with Mrs. Noss.

I told him I was curious about one thing. Was his group

putting up the money as a kind of gambler's speculation?

"It's no speculation," he replied. "A few weeks ago I was in a small town in Texas and I saw twenty-two old gold bars that came from the Noss cave, about 6 million dollars worth. I counted the bars myself."

It was their plan, he said, to arrange for federal authorities to seize the gold, file a title suit and hopefully win the case for the Noss family as the rightful owner; this in turn would produce a handsome fortune for Mrs. Noss and the syndicate.

Ova was anxious to conclude the negotiations, so we gave the syndicate a 15-day option in return for $2,000. Mrs. Noss would sign the primary contract upon a payment to her of the $25,000. Next we met at the Clovis National Bank, where a Walton representative produced a cashier's check for the $25,000. The amiable bank president, Mr. Moody, accepted it and forthwith deposited it to Ova's account.

Far into that night the lights were bright in Ova's little trailer home as daughters Letha and Dorothy toasted mama on her latest triumph. The next day I had an opportunity to discuss with daughter Letha the wisdom of Ova accepting any future offers for a percentage of her interest, again for the obvious reason that difficult as it might be to calculate, Ova might not have anything more to sell. Letha agreed. Ova looked to the $5,000-a-month payments as the dawn of a beautiful new day. Prosperity she had never known was about to enrich her life.

But it was not to be.

The group failed to make its first monthly payment of $5,000. After several written notices to the attorney, I sent a registered letter to Walton declaring the contract null and void.

Now it seemed prudent to reach Walton if for no other reason than to determine whether the group had any knowledge of the contract's cancellation. Their attorney advised he was not able to shed any light on the situation.

He seemed hesitant to explain, and I assumed he may have broken contact with the group.

While these efforts were in progress, Ova came into possession of a stock certificate issued by a Victoria Peak mining corporation. The certificate was signed by a Brent Bauer as secretary and John E. Walton as president. The formation of such a corporation, we learned, was part of the 51%-49% contract between the Walton group and Ova Noss, and was designed to hold the Noss treasure trove as its principal asset. Now, with the contract legally dead, it was important for the Walton group to recognize that the corporation was invalid also. In letters to Walton and Bauer, I expressed the hope I was not being unduly apprehensive that "putting stock certificates of this nature into existence creates certain serious problems." I urged them "to destroy the certificates and retrieve any that may have been disposed of."

Nothing more was ever heard from Walton or the group and we assumed, correctly, the stock certificates were eventually recaptured and destroyed.

Still, there was some consolation for Ova; she had her 49% back and was $25,000 richer.

Another offer, this one from a wholly unexpected source, entered the picture in mid-June of '73.

Expeditions Unlimited, a Florida corporation, made what appeared to be a very attractive proposal. It would contract to undertake all preliminary work and pay all the expenses for the recovery of Ova's treasure. Norman Scott, president of E.U., demonstrated to our satisfaction that his company had a fine record in the art of tracking down lost treasures, sunken ships and such, and selling the story in movie, book and TV markets.

No monies would change hands under such an arrangement. Expeditions Unlimited would derive its fees from a share of the treasures, provided its efforts at recovery were successful.

Scott suggested the following division, after all expenses were deducted:

Gold bullion: 15% to E.U. - 85% to Mrs. Noss

Jewels, coins: 25% to E.U. - 75% to Mrs. Noss

Artifacts: 25% to E.U. - 75% to Mrs. Noss

Books, TV, Movies, etc: 75% to E.U. - 25% to Mrs. Noss

Quickly, our early discussions indicated a meeting between Scott and the Noss family was in order, and one was set for June 26 in Clovis.

On the 25th, my wife Mary and I were enroute to Clovis by motor car and had put in at a motel in western Kansas in the early afternoon, in deference to an unusually hot sun and fatigue from an early morning start. A small outdoor pool beckoned to Mary while I hastened to the television set, remembering that on this day, the 25th of June, John W. Dean, President Nixon's White House counsel, was to testify before the Senate Watergate committee.

Dean, who would serve four months in prison for his central role in the cover-up, was on the stand, responding to questions from the committee chairman, Sam Ervin.

Then, with startling suddeness, he volunteered a piece of information that seemed totally unrelated to the Watergate conspiracy. He related that back in March he was at a luncheon meeting with Attorney General John N. Mitchell and Nixon's Chief of Staff, H. R. Haldeman. In the course of the conversation, Dean said Mitchell turned to Haldeman and said: "A friend of ours, F. Lee Bailey, has a problem he would like some help on. He has some clients who have an enormous amount of gold in their possession and would like to make an arrangement with the government. His clients want to turn the gold over to the government and not be prosecuted for hoarding the gold."

Haldeman did not respond or comment and the conversation turned to other matters.

The newspapers had a field day, having ascertained that the gold referred to by Bailey had come from the White Sands Missile range area. Stories about the Noss lost-treasure appeared on front pages all over the country. Tremors crackled through the ranks of treasure trove claimants of all sizes and origin.

By the next day reporters had ferreted out the key details of Bailey's behind-the-scenes maneuver. There was no denial that the gold claimed by the Bailey clients came from the Victoria Peak area, though a somewhat aggressive effort was made to place the location of their gold at some distance from that of the Noss treasure.

Bailey told reporters he represented fifty persons in all. He would not disclose their names, "now or ever." He said forty were "finders" who lived in the White Sands area and "know the exact location of the gold." The other ten clients were businessmen willing to act as middlemen in a sale of the gold.

"In my opinion the clients are telling the truth," he told the Albuquerque Tribune reporter Howard Bryan in a telephone interview, in which Bailey made other disclosures:

> When he contacted the White House, Bailey was asked to get a Treasury department assay of the gold. He furnished a small bar of gold that proved to be 60% gold, 40% copper, and "very old."
>
> Bailey then wrote the Department of the Army requesting formal permission to enter the Missile Range and claim the gold. His request had gone unanswered. He planned to go to court to force entry into the range on the basis the finders have property rights in the gold.
>
> The gold bar furnished for assay was given to him by one of his clients who, he said, did not pick it up on the Missile Range but had gotten it elsewhere.
>
> Bailey expressed fear that gold was being stolen from the Missile Range.

He said his clients saw some people take two tons of gold from White Sands in two jeeps and a truck. This was reported to the Assistant Secretary of the Treasury. No action was taken. The identities of those in the jeeps and truck were known to witnesses. They were not military people.

Bailey was prepared to deliver 292 bars of gold to the government, if he could gain access to the Missile Range. That number, he said, represented only a small part of the total gold.

"What we have there is 100 tons of gold worth $250 million," Bailey told Bryan.

In addition to the gold, Bailey said his clients are claiming "many old artifacts and a multitude of coins in old leather pouches," and did not discount the idea that the gold and coins came from a mine in southern New Mexico.

Bailey disclosed he was told by government officials that there is a "very thick file" on a lot of treasure claims on the White Sands Missile Range which were investigated and which never proved out. "But they never yet have had people who claim to know the exact location of gold with the specific amount and specific form." (Obviously, Bailey was not aware of Colonel Fiege's discovery in 1958 of the cache of gold bars at Victoria Peak.)

Bailey complained:

"Why can't they spare me thirty minutes and a helicopter to show them I know what I am talking about?"

When his clients first broached their problem, Bailey suggested that they take him to the site so he could view the gold. He assured them he would be able to obtain permission from the government. The group refused, fearing such a mission might jeopardize their title to the gold and most certainly would disclose its location.

139

It was then that Bailey in mid-March called upon John Mitchell, fully four months before Dean's Watergate testimony.

When Haldeman proved unresponsive, Mitchell reported back to Bailey that he might see presidential advisor John Erlichman. A series of contacts with the Treasury Department followed, and ultimately Bailey reached the office of Thomas W. Wolfe, Office of Domestic Gold and Silver Operations.

According to *Time* magazine, Wolfe bluntly told Bailey his clients were "full of malarkey". Wolfe brushed off the attorney with a tart reminder that any gold discovery must be reported to the Secret Service; he then offered a less than heartfelt suggestion that Bailey ask the Army for special permission to go upon the Missile Range and locate the gold.

The Treasury Department's own analysis of the bar of gold secured by Bailey showed that it contained 60% gold, but in spite of that tantalizing bit of evidence Bailey's plea for permission to pick up the treasure drew no response from the government.

There was no lack of interest or speculation in the Noss quarters. Bailey had mentioned a specific number of bars — 292. How had his clients come into that figure? Had they made their way onto the site and to the cache? How otherwise could they have come into possession of the single "ancient" bar produced by Bailey for assay?

Even among the non-believers, notably the Treasury and Defense departments, evidence of the existence of a treasure seemed to be mounting to a point almost impossible to refute. Looking back on the extraordinary number of events one might be hard-pressed to accept General Shinkle's conclusion, "There is not a damn thing to it."

Reactions to the Bailey disclosures were numerous and emotional.

Ova Noss had heard John Dean's TV testimony on the

25th. She was excited and irritated; it was fine that an attorney of F. Lee Bailey's reputation was now, in a sense, a Noss supporter but, she insisted, "they have no claim at all to the gold. It belongs to us."

Despite prods from one source or another, Bailey held to his decision not to reveal the identities of his clients. He told the press he had sent a formal request to Army headquarters in Washington to allow his people to go upon the Missile Range and recover the gold bars. He then revealed the government had made a claim for 50% of whatever treasure was found, including that possessed by Bailey's clients.

The percentage-demand provoked a heated reply from the Commissioner's office in Santa Fe, via its attorney Oscar Jordan, rejecting the federal government's claim to any mineral or mining products on the Range. Once again Jordan referred to lease provisions restricting the Army's right to use *only* the surface of the ground, nothing more. He contended that if any governmental body had a right to a percentage of the gold it would be the State of New Mexico as owner of the land. Further, if Bailey wanted upon the Missile Range, he would most certainly have to obtain a permit also from the Land Office.

The visit in Clovis now included a pre-arranged meeting with officials of Expeditions Unlimited. There we told them that any decision on their offer to take over for the Noss family had to be tabled for the time being.

After two days of meetings I decided Ova Noss should move on two separate fronts — a lawsuit for $1 billion against three parties — the State of New Mexico, the federal government and "100 John Does" — to be filed in federal court in Albuquerque. Secondly, a formal statement reciting the Noss family's historical claim to the gold and entered into Land Office records.

The legal action was filed late in August. It cited Ova

Noss' claim to 100% ownership of a treasure "in gold, coins and antiquities valued in excess of $1 billion" and asked the court to direct the defendants to allow her to go upon the range and remove her property. Besides the two governments named in our petition, the other defendants — "100 John Does" — were Bailey's unidentified clients and other interested clients.

My own 2-page statement to the Land Office on June 28 covered mostly old ground, summarizing the history of the trove from the point of Doc Noss' discovery in 1937 to Ova's 18 years' "open possession" with official state permission.

The statement said in part:

"For approximately eighteen years prior to July 23, 1955, Ova Noss and members of her family had been in open possession of Victoria Peak and surrounding land in said Section 16.

"On or about July 23, 1955, representatives of the United States Army forcibly and without due process of law evicted the plaintiffs and members of her family from the area. Prior to that time the United States had affected a condemnation of several tracts of land to comprise what is known as the White Sands Missile Range, which surrounds Victoria Peak and Section 16, but in none of these comdemnation actions was the Noss family joined as a party.

"Through the years the successive commanders of the base have excluded Mrs. Noss from Victoria Peak and frustrated several efforts on her part to obtain permission to go onto the base and recapture the gold and artifacts.

"At various times and dates, some known to Mrs. Noss, members of the armed forces have wrongfully explored the area and seized a part of the personal property belonging to the Noss family, especially quantities of gold bars. They have broken into shafts and entrances made by the Noss family and closed and locked by them at the time they were wrongfully ejected by agents of the United States Army.

"The Noss family will take the appropriate steps to bring about a proper resolution of the question of ownership to the gold alluded to by the group represented by Mr. F. Lee Bailey, and further will petition both the Federal and New Mexico governments to permit entry of Noss family representatives upon the White Sands Missile base to permit them to possess and remove personal property rightfully theirs."

Mrs. Noss, son Marvin and daughter Letha had met me in Santa Fe, all checking in at the Desert Inn motel across the street from the Land Office. The next morning we gathered for breakfast at the motel, in the course of which I observed a gentleman seated nearby seemingly intent on the conversation at our table. More than an hour was consumed in a discussion with Brent Bauer, who had initiated our talks with the Walton group in Salt Lake City. Still the stranger watched, seated in an open position toward our table. Finally, I asked Bauer whether the man was a friend of his or a member of his party.

"Not at all," Bauer said. "He belongs to a syndicate in Los Angeles that black markets gold. He goes wherever there is a chance for the syndicate to buy it. He'll trail you folks around for months and when he feels the time is ripe he'll move in with his offer."

From that point on, when possible, we met behind closed doors but I still kept a wary eye out for the black marketeer.

Early in July I wrote to the then Commander of the White Sands Missile Range, Maj. Gen. Arthur H. Sweeney, Jr. stating in part:

I feel it unnecessary to press the point of the extent of anxiety of the Noss family throughout the years over the treasure trove which they deeply and most convincingly feel is present there. Their requests for re-entry have been denied them and they await the opportunity in the future, however long it may take.

Consequently, one may well imagine their feelings upon hearing the reading that the F. Lee Bailey group is petitioning high sources in Washington, D. C., to allow them to enter upon the base and recover, in their words, "292 bars of gold hidden in a cave on White Sands."

We urge you to exert whatever influence is appropriate to your Command toward the impounding of such treasure so that a proper judicial forum can be established, and thus give opportunity to claimants, whoever they may be, to plead their respective cause.

General Sweeney's reply:

Dear Mr. Koury:

This is in reply to your letter of 5 July 1973 concerning the Noss mining claim.

You ask in your letter that this Command take action to have a treasure trove allegedly located on White Sands Missile Range impounded in order that various claimants to the treasure trove can litigate their claims. This is to inform you that there is no known treasure trove existing on White Sands Missile Range. Furthermore, there is no exploration or probing of the Noss mine claim on or near Victoria Peak.

It has been the consistent policy of this Command to deny requests for entry on the range for purposes of exploration for treasure or gold. No evidence has been presented which would warrant a departure from this policy and it is my intent to adhere to this course of action unless directed to the contrary by higher competent authority.

144

At this point, our thoughts centered on the fact the Bailey clients and the Noss family had a common objective — to get their hands on the treasure trove. Both sides were uncertain as to what legal process would intervene should they decide to move separately, apart from the remote possibility that rights of ownership might go to a third party. A court hearing appeared to be the surest way to determine the legal owner, in which case it was wiser for the Bailey and Noss groups to move hand-in-hand legally.

Accordingly, we favored a joint effort, further encouraged by the obvious fact that, in the event of a division of the treasure, there was more than enough to satisfy the appetites of both groups.

National news services and the larger metropolitan dailies were calling my office almost daily, inquiring about developments. Since I had had no contact thus far with F. Lee Bailey personally, the Associated Press quoted me in an article in which I revealed a plan to meet with Bailey and within a few days I received a telephone call from Bailey's law associate, Al Johnson, suggesting a meeting with Bailey and other serious claimants.

There were indeed other serious claimants.

Through the years some had been consistently vocal. Others became more assertive after Dean's TV testimony and the resurgence of publicity about the Noss claim.

The claimants

Roscoe W. Parr, a Texan, was probably the most impressive — and aloof — of all the claimants. In a quiet way he had informed the Land Office through the years that he possessed a right which he could legally establish, entitling him to at least two-thirds of the Noss treasures. He claimed to have begun his friendship with Doc Noss in 1941, assisting him in the effort to regain access to the treasure trove, and to have continued the relationship until Doc's death in 1949. He described himself as a close personal friend and full partner. Legal counsel had assured him it was valid.

Further, Parr let it be known, Doc Noss had given him specific instructions as to what actions should be taken upon his death. He would not disclose the exact nature of the instructions but said he would be present at any proceeding involving the Army, State of New Mexico or Court of law.

In late August '73, Parr's attorney, W. Doyle Elliott, made a plea to the Land Office to view Parr's claim "as important as Mrs. Noss'." He repeated his contention that Parr "is the only person living today who has the instructions, information and directions that Doc Noss possessed."

Later, Elliott advised Governor King that "in light of the request of Mr. Bailey for immunity from criminal prosecution for one or more of his clients, we are of the belief that Mr. Bailey's clients have gained access to the treasure trove and have taken possession of a part of it .... The instructions that Mr. Parr received from Doc

Noss should be given consideration at least equal to that being given to Bailey's claim to $26,500,000 in gold bars, even though Bailey can deliver such gold. Mr. Parr has the key to much more."

Elliott requested that he and Parr be allowed to go along in the event Bailey is permitted upon the site to pinpoint the location of the 292 bars.

In her swashbuckling attitude toward any competing interest, Ova advised me that "Doc Noss gave Parr nothing."

Parr's name does appear in numerous old documents, mostly affidavits, involving assignments of interests by Doc Noss; many are on file in the Land Office. More significantly his name is among groups who on various occasions during Noss' lifetime organized formal ventures aimed at re-opening the old shaft, or in solicitations for funds to finance a needed improvement at Victoria Peak. There seemed little doubt Parr would have to be reckoned with in any substantive judgment involving the treasure trove.

The most obvious claim, though possibly the most complex legally, was that of Doc's widow, Violet Noss Yancy. At the time Parr was restating his position at the Land Office, Attorney Jack W. Beech of Fort Worth, Texas, was advising both the Army department and the Land Office that any move which did not include his client, Mrs. Yancy, would compel him to take legal steps. Not unlike other claimants, he would object to any unilateral government-supervised probe by the Bailey group, but would be happy to take part in a collective effort involving all qualified claimants.

Ova, not the negotiating type when it came to the treasure, rejected out of hand any notion of Violet Yancy's eligibility: Doc Noss' divorce was illegal and consequently so was Violet's marriage to him. At no time did Mrs. Yancy assert she knew where the treasure cavern or any cache of gold was located, asking only that she be dealt with fairly as the finder's surviving widow.

The most mysterious among the claimants was Fred Drolte of El Paso. He represented not only himself but a few others, unnamed. Preferring to remain in the background, he would send a representative to any gathering of claimants, he himself issuing instructions usually from a nearby hotel room. An article about the treasure trove in the Dec. 18, 1975, issue of *Rolling Stone,* describes Drolte as a semi-recluse . . . "He's got a semi-barricaded existence. He's not listed in the phone books or city directory . . . he claims he's touched the gold."

We were aware of other individuals with claims, though there was little in the records about them. In a few instances the individual was acting on behalf of a consortium, its members usually unnamed, as in the case of the Bailey group.

At various times we heard reports that Bailey's clients had joined hands with the Drolte group and an even less visible claimant, Joe Newman. But Newman advised the Army that no such association existed, that he was proceeding on his own. It was understood that Drolte was a key figure in the Bailey setup, some observers even insisting that Drolte was one of the fifty clients. And further that he was among a few claimants who early in the relationship did not want Bailey to see any of the gold bars.

In any event, it appeared to be a nervous association. The Bailey group admitted that without Drolte they had no guide to the specific cave entrance. Bailey himself added a somewhat strange note. "Besides," he said, "there are men at the peak with high-powered rifles. Drolte's team. That's why I didn't go out alone. I had no white flag to get past those rifles and no idea where to go."

In mid-1974 Drolte advised the Army by letter that the

Bailey-Drolte group "wanted to work in two sections, 16 and 22," in its effort to recover the treasures. He included a chart setting out his version of the respective interest of several claimants in whatever may be recovered, as follows:

STATE OF NEW MEXICO	UNITED STATES GOVERNMENT
25%	25%

All expenses such as removal, security, assaying, etc.

F. LEE BAILEY 10%

FRED P. DROLTE 60%	E. D. PATTERSON 40%
DON FURR, et al 10% of 60%	FRANK SAINZ 10% of 40%
W. E. SWENSON 10% of 60%	WAYNE LAWSON 10% of 40%
W. T. DURANT 10% of 60%	

Drolte further disclosed he was the one who furnished Bailey with the gold bar that was assayed by the U. S. Treasury, and was later reported to contain 60% gold and, according to the carbon-date testing, was more than 300 years old.

Obviously, there had been secret visits to Victoria Peak — without official permit or knowledge. It was indeed a facet in the treasure syndrome which few cared to deny and many suspected; it was simply taken for granted many clandestine excursions to the peak had been made in the intervening years.

In fact, early in '62 one of the attorneys in our own group was suddenly affected with a high spirit of derring-do. Over the strong objections of co-counsel he joined two friends of the Noss family one night, and properly attired in khaki and studded boots, drove to a point on a road bordering the Missile Range. There the party vaulted the wire fence and began a walk of five or six hours to the peak. Reach it they did, and peering over the ridge some hundred yards distant they saw Victoria's gray, furrowed face. They returned to their vehicle just as the dawn began to shed its light, exhausted but jubilant over the success of the adventure.

Among the daring sallies that marked the career of the troubled desert melodrama it is certain few were less productive or more inadequately planned than this one by my co-counsel, though we were momentarily impressed by his rhapsodic allusions to the peak "in its solitary, austere magnificence."

It is impossible to count or classify how many other claimants waited in the wings for a judical forum — or any other kind of hearing — in which to plead their specific case. We knew that some had claims as little as 1/10th of 1%, obtained mostly through agreements with Doc or Ova Noss, and were spiritedly prepared to exhibit their proof — often by way of documents yellow with age and barely legible.

A man named William R. Newhall of Pinellas County, Florida, filed an affidavit with the Department of the Army stating he owned almost 24% of the Shriver interest and was therefore entitled to any information about "the White Sands treasure trove." The W. William Shriver group was destined to be included in the Army's list of "qualified claimants" who would be considered in any plan to enter the Missile Range. Others at the moment: Ova Noss, Violet Yancy, Roscoe Parr, the Bailey and Drolte groups.

There were other claimants who notified various authorities of their interest in the treasure trove following John Dean's testimony:

A. D. Black of Norman, Oklahoma: Says he

bought an interest in the Noss mine in 1953 for $5,000 from Ova Noss.

Dale K. Pepper, Lubbock, Texas: "I spent several weeks out there in 1941 cleaning out loose silt and rocks from the mine shaft on Victoria Peak .... some of the things Doc Noss had in his possession made me believe strongly in the possibility of there being some truth about these treasures."

Charles E. Wolfe, South Haven, Kansas: Says he was assigned 1% of Ova Noss' interest "in the treasure, minerals and other things of value .... these assignments were given for valuable consideration."

D. F. Berggren, Arkansas City, Kansas: Holds 1% of the 100% of Ova Noss' "original interest after state and legal settlements are made in the purported treasure."

Mary Jane Perry, Albuquerque, New Mexico: States in a notarized affidavit to the Land Office that the family of the late Teofil Van Dame, Sr., claims an undivided ⅓ interest "to any and all treasures recovered from Victoria Peak." The affidavit lists ten persons as family members and beneficiaries.

Antonio S. Candelaria, Las Cruces, New Mexico: His letter with the Land Office lists nine persons as claimants, stating .... "there is a cave which contains two caches, one immediately to the left and one farther inside the cave."

Joe Ray Williams, Albuquerque: His letter to the Land Office claims the entire treasure on behalf of the Alamo band of Indians on the theory they are "the descendants of the Apache tribe .... this treasure has been historically related to ancient Apaches such as Victorio, Nana and others who as a nation fought Spanish and American governments during the era this treasure was collected."

Eugene W. Waltrip, Arkansas City, Kansas, claims he and Herbert F. Jimmerson own 1% of Mrs. Noss' interest, sold by her in the 1950's. Payment was to be used "as grubstake money and to repair the road up Victoria Peak."

Numerous persons called our office offering services of extraordinary variety. One gentleman assured us he possessed a "twig technique" by which he could ascertain the location of the treasure merely by waving his special branch above the ground in the approximate area. He would accept a fee only in the event his probe was successful.

Another described himself as a friend of the Apache Indians and asked to be commissioned to circulate among the Indians in the Southwest and would draw from them the secret of Chief Victorio, whom he viewed as the true owner of the treasure.

A crystal gazer, a sun worshipper, a numerology expert (he was certain Ova's birthdate would yield the answer), and an aged mystic were among those with tenders of foolproof solutions.

Not all, however, were interested in helping us locate the gold or in establishing their own claims. There were a few who wanted in *after* the gold was found. The most spectacular of this genre was a group of individuals professing contacts with the movie industry. Their initial call was made to Ova, and their offer ($300,000 in "front money") struck her as attractive enough to cause her and members of her family to keep a rendezvous in Garden Grove, California.

It was mid-August and our office was talking to Bailey and other claimants to set a date and place for a general conference on mutual problems.

A call came in from Ova. "You don't know about this but we got a fella who is going to bring in some big money. We need a contract."

"What kind of contract?"

"Something that he can use to get us a movie contract about the treasure. Here, I'll put him on the phone."

He began by saying there was an excellent chance he could sell the movie rights to the Noss story. "I need a power of attorney," he said.

I told him that was out of the question. Instead I agreed to prepare a limited agency document effective for one month only, giving him the right to sell the movie rights only with our prior approval of the terms.

The following day I received a call from the spokesman from an airport somewhere in Texas; he would not say where. We reviewed the conversation of the day before and I assured him I would have the agency contract to him in a day or two.

The Nosses called. They were resentful; the spokesman had promised he would have $300,000 in hand when they arrived in Garden Grove, and he did not have the cash. Further, they did not think he was in a position to produce any "front" or "lead" money. And without it there could be no deal. Ova agreed with my suggestion that we offer the following terms: A down payment of $50,000 at the signing, $100,000 thirty days later and $150,000 when the treasure is in hand.

The spokesman for the group did not take to the offer kindly. He said the terms were too severe and probably would "kill the deal."

He phoned again the next day, hoping for a change in our position. I insisted he advise his principals that the conditions were firm. Nothing further was heard from him. I telephoned Ova and again emphasized the sensitive nature of the circumstances.

Though somewhat more elaborate, this latest offer for a "piece of the action without any front money", as Ova put it, was not the first of the kind.

In each such overtures there was an element of potential fraud which caused us much concern.

For example, an individual somehow comes into possession of gold bars, possibly through illegal means. It is a burden that has to be dealt with, so the party approaches a member of the Noss family. He does not disclose he has the gold in hand, but he says he knows where he can get his hands on some gold bars and is willing to turn them over to the Nosses — if they will share the value of the gold with him on a 50-50 basis. This arrangement gives him a profitable outlet for his contraband and at the same time enables him to escape the clutches of the law. And it is attractive to the Noss family as an expedient opportunity to acquire gold without expenditure of effort or money.

After a few contacts of this caliber, we became convinced that unsavory elements were attempting to weave their way into the picture. We suspected there were also fringe operators tied in with black-market purveyors who were keeping a close watch on our progress.

On one occasion a "front man" approached the Noss family with a plan that would enable them to recapture gold bars taken from the Noss cave.

He explained how it would work:

He would buy a few bars of gold from certain individuals who, he knew, possessed a large number of them. He would pay the asking price and when he got the confidence of the possessors, he would persuade them to show him the bulk of their gold. Whereupon he and his confederates would physically seize the gold and claim it on the theory that all of it belonged to the Noss family. The drama would reach its telling climax with the demand that the possessors negotiate . . . or else. Thus stripped of all options, the possessors would agree to turning over one-half to the Noss family.

His fee for engineering this brilliant *coup de matre:* a reasonable share of the Noss family's one-half.

The in-fighting

By late '73 the embattled Noss treasure trove was enmeshed in claims, counterclaims, in numerous maneuvers for preferential position. There was little concert of action.

Fierce in-fighting was taking place among claimants like Newman, Drolte, Parr and Bailey — not to mention the Nosses. Within the official New Mexico family, the Commissioner of Lands office was quietly challenging the right of the Attorney General's office to make any agreement affecting the treasure.

On the other hand, all New Mexico officials, including Governor King and the Land Office people, were staunchly on the side of the claimants in their struggle with the U. S. Army. This hostility was deepened when the Army announced it would claim 50% of whatever treasure came out of Victoria Peak.

At this stage, even though the Command at White Sands had placed a permanent ban on any further exploration at the Peak, Army brass in Washington appeared to be relaxing a little; there were indications a re-entry upon the Range would be permitted if a plan could be devised that would be "fair to all the clients and preferential to no single client."

Still, it was obvious the Army had no particular plan in mind. And it was distracted at the moment by Bailey, who was banging at its door and crying out for a permit. In a transparent stall for time it advised him by letter it would *consider* his request to go upon the Range if he did two things: Reveal the names of all his clients and the location of the gold.

Bailey bristled.

"I am not about to reveal the names of my clients so that they can be harassed by the Army," he told the press angrily. "And I am not about to tell the location of the gold so that the Army's weekend treasure hunters can go looking for it."

The letter to Bailey, signed by an Assistant Secretary of the Army, George Brazier, repeated the Army's position on the Missile Range, pointing out that for twenty years it has denied such requests, the only exception made in 1963 when a mining company was allowed to search for legendary gold under authority granted to the Museum of New Mexico, which effort produced no gold. "Your request differs from the norm in that you claim to know exactly where gold bullion is located and seek permission not to explore but merely to enter the Missile Range so that the alleged gold bullion may be removed. Nevertheless, you have as yet presented no cogent reason why an exception to the Army's policy of exclusion should be made in your case, or why the Army should reach a decision favorable to you without first being advised of the names of all your clients and the location of the alleged gold bullion in terms precise enough to permit the Army to determine its jurisdiction over the alleged gold bullion area."

Bailey called the Army's position asinine and announced he would take his case to the state of New Mexico. The state, he said, has some rights to the treasures through its ownership of land within the White Sands complex.

In a meeting with Gov. Bruce King shortly thereafter Bailey gave a comprehensive analysis of his group's position. The Governor, openly sympathetic, concurred with the legal steps being considered, and advised that his office would publicly support Bailey's efforts to obtain an entry permit.

Bailey had commented to Governor King that his clients were not greedy; they would be happy to share a percentage of the treasure with the state. But there were some preliminary legal steps that had to be taken.

The first of these was an immunity agreement with the state, signed by Attorney General David L. Norvell.

Under its terms, Bailey agreed to compile a list of the names and social security numbers of his clients. The list would then be sealed and placed in a depository (in the Bank of Santa Fe). Access to it could be had only by Bailey. A document was prepared and executed, in which the state agreed it would not prosecute any of the persons named in the list for possession of gold or artifacts taken from the Victoria Peak area.

In late January, as a sort of "thank you for the immunity", Bailey signed a second contract by which his group gave the State of New Mexico 25% of its share of the treasure. In that document the treasure was described "as certain valuable treasure trove, mineral deposits, bullion, coins, historical artifacts and precious or semi-precious stones and unmined precious mineral deposits".

Not unexpectedly, the two Bailey-Norvell agreements drew angry reactions from several of the major claimants and within a few weeks produced a move that was inevitable; the offended claimants took the issue to court.

With sweeping charges, Ova Noss herself was the first to go on record in the Santa Fe state district court. Her petition, filed by special counsel Paul G. Bardacke of Albuquerque, challenged Norvell's right to make such an agreement with the Bailey group, contending that New Mexico statutes assigned that power to the Commissioner of Lands office.

Referring to them as "John Does 1 through 50", the Noss petition accused unnamed defendants of going upon Victoria Peak, taking possession of her personal property and "through stealth relocating and hiding it." Further, she contended that a legal disability rendered the Bailey-Norvell agreement invalid; the provisions giving Bailey clients immunity from prosecution in exchange for a 25% share in the Noss treasures, she contended, constituted an infringement upon public policy.

Finally, she condemned the agreement as a violation of her rights under the U. S. Constitution on the basis it deprived her of property without due process of law.

Next, Violet F. Yancy took a turn at litigation.

In a complaint filed in the same state court she asked that she be declared the owner of the Noss treasure and of any part taken from the site.

One of the documents included with the petition brought to light a contract which we, as Ova's counsel, did not know existed, and which Ova had never mentioned to us. It was a contract entered into in 1944 by which Doc Noss gave Ova "24% of the 100% of the net recovery from the treasures or minerals found on state lease lands and patented lands owned by Jack Bruton in the San Andres mountains of New Mexico". (The petition assumed these locations were within the Victoria Peak area.)

Ova's case against the state and F. Lee Bailey's clients was heard by Judge Santiago E. Campos in early August of '74, with Bailey and other defense attorneys presenting arguments.

In its decree the court took official notice of the list of Bailey's clients which it had ordered placed in a safety deposit box. It instructed Bailey not to remove or transfer the list without the court's permission. The court further ordered the parties "to go forth to the site of the treasure," recover it and put it in the custody of a court-appointed receiver, Jack M. Campbell of Santa Fe.

The ruling was something of a shock — a state court

ordering entry upon land leased by and under the jurisdiction of the U. S. government.

That afternoon of the same day, Norvell sent a lengthy wire to the Secretary of the Army, Howard H. Callaway, advising him of Judge Campos' decision and requesting that the Army give Receiver Campbell "permission to enter Victoria Peak at once."

Callaway's wired reply was brief and to the point: "Your request . . . is denied."

Norvell was not unaware of the specifications earlier laid down by the Army — claimants would be permitted to enter the Range under a 48-hour license if they name their clients and reveal the approximate location of the treasure.

Now, perhaps unwittingly, he had backed the Army into a corner by asking for preferential treatment for the Drolte-Bailey group.

In a further comment, Secretary Callaway accused the Drolte-Bailey group of trying to be the first ones on the peak "merely because they had in 1973 produced a small bar of metal which contained a substantial proportion of gold and because they had entered into a contract with Mr. Norvell which purportedly gave the state's consent to such entry in return for a promise to pay the State of New Mexico 25% of the value of treasure recovered." It had not been established, Callaway pointed out, that either the bar of metal submitted by Bailey to the Treasury Department for testing in April, 1973 or the different bar of metal submitted by the Drolte-Bailey group last week has any connection with lost treasure or White Sands Missile Range.

"The Norvell-Bailey contract does not appear to entitle the Drolte-Bailey group to any preferential treatment. As a result, I regard the Drolte-Bailey group as entitled to only the same treatement accorded other applicants seeking permission to remove the treasure, all of whom state unequivocally that they know exactly where the treasure is located."

Dissention among the parties had now reached a new high:

The Army in Washington, taking the initiative, was overruling the Commanding Officer at White Sands.

The New Mexico Land Office and the Attorney General were in an internal dispute over jurisdiction.

New Mexico resented - and would not accept - the Army's decision that it was not necessary to obtain an entry permit from the state. Further, it rejected the Army's claim to 50% of the treasure trove as wholly untenable.

New Mexico and the U. S. Army were figuratively glaring at each other in their respective roles as landlord and tenant.

As owner of the land New Mexico viewed the Army's claim to any part of the treasure, much less 50%, as a brazen attempt to get something to which it was not legally entitled. After all, under the lease terms the Army could use only the surface of the ground. Embarking on mining activities without the state's consent — or knowledge — or laying claim to precious minerals found on the Missile Range struck the state as more than a lease violation; it was at least trespass and possibly unlawful appropriation of another's property.

To establish its position New Mexico decided to take court action immediately. Suddenly, the thrust of the treasure trove controversy moved to a higher level; for the moment the confused medley of personal claims was pushed into the background.

In mid-August of '74, Attorney General David L. Norvell, acting for the state, went into federal district court in Albuquerque with a complaint naming as defendants three U. S. officials — Secretary of the Army Callaway; Deputy General Counsel of the Army Bland

West, and Robert J. Proudfoot, Commanding General, White Sands Missile Range.

In his petition plaintiff Norvell stated he is "informed and believes" there is property on or under the Victoria Peak area "consisting of gold bullion, coins, historical artifacts . . . . including 18,000 gold bars more or less" and that such property is still there "unless it has been removed by the defendants . . . . or persons acting in concert with them."

(It was the first *official* disclosure of the approximate number of gold bars purportedly in the original caverns. The Noss family had repeatedly expressed the belief there were many thousands of bars "stacked like cord wood", but no estimate of the number had been publicly stated. The state's estimate prompted Ova in later years to put the value of the entire treasure at more than a billion dollars.)

The Norvell petition asked the court to:

• Compel the Army to allow the State of New Mexico to enter the Range and retrieve the treasure.

• Place the treasure in the hands of a Receiver so that various claims of ownership might be adjudicated.

• Order the Army to stop its agents from conducting illegal searches at Victoria Peak.

• Take official notice of the fact the Army is presently contracting with third parties to recover and remove the treasure in exchange for a part interest.

In its reply to the petition, the Army challenged the state's right to bring such a lawsuit, asked the court to dismiss the complaint.

Five months later Judge Howard Bratton rendered a mixed judgment settling most of the key issues.

He ruled:

• The Army has no right to probe the Missile Range for treasure trove.

• The State of New Mexico has no right of entry without the Army's permission.

• The commander of the Missile Range has the discretion to permit or deny entry upon the Range. And may deny a permit to any claimant who seeks preferential treatment over other claimants.

• Entry onto the Range requires the permission of both the state and the Army.

The court then indulged itself in a somewhat whimsical summary:

"The case grows out of the long-lasting legend that there is located somewhere on Victoria Peak a vast treasure of gold bars, jewels, and valuable artifacts. It has been claimed that certain people have been in the cave where the treasure is located and have seen the treasure. From time to time, the legend is revived, and public interest in the matter increases. There apparently are some people, or groups of people, within whom interest has been sustained, for the Army has regularly had contacts with such people and requests from them for permission to seek and remove the treasure. Hoping to finally put the subject to rest, the Army in 1963 permitted a state-sponsored expedition to go onto the range and conduct an exploration. The expedition's efforts proved fruitless. They found nothing. The legend was more durable than empirical data tending to show its chimerical nature, and, in the recent past, substantial interest in it forced the Army to begin exploring terms and conditions upon which competing groups could be allowed onto the range to look for the treasure."

Judge Bratton's ruling produced a kind of Mexican stand-off. It did, however, clear the path to processing requests to enter the Missile Range. Now, definitely, the permission of both governments was required.

The state was ready and willing, not so the Army and Defense departments. But even those quarters were grudgingly approaching a point of decision. The clamor of claimants was now spirited and persistent, their demands daily growing more legally sophisticated. Still,

162

the Army did not entertain the slightest intention of surrendering totally. One possibility they must avoid: An Oklahoma-like land rush of claimants and crews dashing helter-skelter onto the Victoria Peak area, with the grim prospect of violence among the "prospectors" in the style of Western movies.

Not long after the Bratton decision, the Defense department announced it would shortly issue a "plan of re-entry" to approved claimants. Almost as a footnote it delivered a stern ultimatum: This would be the last time exploration at the Missile Range would be permitted.

The Army moved into the task with a vengeance. Fairness would reign supreme. No presumption would be indulged in any claimant's favor. No preference, not the slightest. Once the ground rules were established, compliance down to the smallest detail would be expected.

We began to wonder whether this attitude would produce a plan so tightly entwined with conditions and limitations as to make it unworkable.

We would soon know.

On August 2, 1974, what Secretary Callaway dubbed "Operation Goldfinder" got underway.

The six principal claimants (Bailey, Parr, Shriver, Noss, Yancy, Drolte) received a packet from the Office of the General Counsel, Department of the Army, Washington D.C., with a covering letter signed by Bland West, Deputy General Counsel, Military and Civil Affairs.

Bland West's approach, then as always, was friendly, considerate, his attitude impressively impartial. However, he let it be known rules were rules and must be observed to the letter.

That was not going to be easy.

Included in the Army's packet was an intricate document, even more intricate than is customary with such documents, setting forth all the rules and regulations that each claimant must follow if he is to be permitted upon the Missile Range. Remarkable in its prolixity, the license document left nothing untouched in the way of conditions and limitations.

Prepared by the Department of the Army on behalf of the U. S. Government, it granted to each claimant a license for a period not exceeding 72 hours. Anyone who was caught on the range for a longer period would be arrested.

Then in cold, unyielding military prose the 2,500-word document sculptured one shackle after another. Restrictions, waivers, stipulations — all in a tone and temper rising to a crescendo of autocratic power.

The arrogantly unilateral terms left all of us dazed and incredulous. In making much of its role as arbiter the Army had made the least of ours as applicants. In effect, it consented to entry, but under conditions almost impossible to accept or even implement.

Here, restated in layman's language, are some of the key provisions:

If any art objects are found, they belong to the United States, and the claimant who finds them gets nothing.

If the government is sued for any reason whatever, the claimant pays all expenses.

Missile testing would go on during the 72 hours the claimants are on the range and if a party is hit by a missile it is not the Army's fault. The injured party will pay all medical and other expenses. Similarly, if a party steps on an unexploded missile or munition of any kind he pays all medical costs. No lawsuit for mutilation or any other injury is permissible.

If a party comes upon a gold mine — gold in its natural state — the finder has no rights to it.

Further, each party must sign a separate document surrendering all rights to any motion pictures, photographic recording or any other documentation of the treasure location and removal activities. Those rights are reserved to the government.

Then a not-too-subtle thrust at integrity:

"The licensee and his agents, servants or employees shall consent to a thorough search of their persons, vehicles, equipment and any other personal property by government security personnel immediately prior to the licensee's departure from the release point, or entry into any cavern, opening, tunnel, cave or aperture in the licensed area, or immediately after the licensee's return to the release point, or emergence from any cavern, opening, tunnel, cave or aperture in the licensed area."

Of the 25 paragraphs contained in the document, the 25th was probably the most puzzling. It referred specifically to the waiver agreements signed by Mrs. Noss in February of 1963, by which she surrendered whatever rights she might possess to sue the United States government "by reason of its alleged unlawful taking and withholding of her personal property." Now, eleven years later, the Army stipulates in a license agreement that the waiver agreement is still valid and effective, and not voided by Mrs. Noss' consent to the license arrangement.

If the Army were seeking a method to elicit swift response, it had found the perfect formula. The more philosophic among the claimants found the license agreement to be singularly lacking in charm and logic. The not-so-tolerant reacted like a bear taunted by hounds.

Now for the first time, no matter how great their differences, the claimants faced an issue on which they could agree totally.

Within a matter of a few days after dispatch of the license notices, attorneys for several of the six claimants gathered in a motel room in Albuquerque. While my notes on the occasion are surprisingly brief and cryptic, I seem to recall that a few claimants took up their post in private rooms elsewhere, and there received periodic reports from their attorneys as the meeting progressed. The gathering itself had its own special climate — quiet and reserved. What sticks in memory is the tension that pervaded the modest, double-bed bedroom that August day in 1974. Fewer than a dozen were present, each seemingly determined to be seen and not heard — a convocation of basically hostile spirits. Most were in shirt sleeves, chair tilted against a bed or wall. No one made an attempt at introductions, except a short, stocky, coatless individual who puffed incessantly on a succession of cigarettes. As I entered the room this person said, almost without turning toward the door, "I'm F. Lee Bailey."

I quickly removed my coat, a gesture which the circumstances seemed to make mandatory. I soon found myself absorbed in Bailey's soft-spoken assault on the profligacy of the Army, Defense department and the White Sands command. Heads nodded in agreement when he denounced the Army's demand for 50% of the treasure trove. I was not able to sort out all the identities but assumed, besides Bailey and Noss, there were representatives of Roscoe Parr, Violet Yancy, Fred Drolte, Newman and Shriver.

With Bailey keynoting the meeting, we discussed the kind of reply that should be made to the Army. Definitely, we were opposed to the Army's selection of a sequential entry upon White Sands, which meant that one claimant group would enter the range, and when its work was done, another would be sent in, and so on until every claimant had had his or her turn. Such a method, we agreed, could not be fair to all; each felt the legality of his claim would be thus endangered by another claimant. No one wanted to give one claimant even the opportunity merely to handle another claimant's gold.

A few felt it possible to go along with the provision requiring us to reveal the names of our principals and the location of the treasure, Bailey's opposition to those conditions notwithstanding. Secretly, we were on the alert for any move that might result in his entering the range first, even if it meant he could make good his promise to haul out a substantial number of gold bars. That fear, needless to say, caused the meeting to labor under a heavy overburden of caution and feigned courtesy. Each of us was determined not to add to Bailey's acknowledged political power and influence.

The day-long meeting produced little in the way of meaningful plans. What was finally agreed upon was the wording of a brief message, wired to Bland West in reply to the Army's license document, as follows:

We agree to a single entry by a party representing all licensees, and that party to be the Receiver (Jack Campbell) appointed by the State Court of New Mexico. All other terms (of the Army's license document) are unacceptable. This message is dictated in the presence of present claimants of record.

About this time, the secretary of the Army, Howard H. Callaway, sent a special report to the White House, reading in part:

It is alleged that a rich store of gold bullion lies hidden somewhere on White Sands Missile Range, in a promontory known as Victoria Peak ... its origin is in the discovery in 1937 by the late Milton C. "Doc" Noss of a vast cavern 300 feet below ground containing stacks of gold bars, a gold crown, remnants of Wells Fargo chests. As to the amount of gold, a figure of 37 tons is often related ...

In 1939, Noss allegedly set off a charge of dynamite

some 170 feet down and accidentally collapsed the tunnel in such a fashion that he could no longer reach the entrance to the cavern . . .

On 5 March 1949, a disappointed backer (one Charles Ryan) who had reportedly invested $28,000 in the search shot Doc Noss dead when Noss failed to keep a promise to deliver some gold bars . . .

The Army has consistently refused to admit persons to White Sands for the purpose of exploring for the alleged treasure. A major exception was made in 1963, when the Museum of New Mexico was granted a permit to search Victoria Peak for possible archaeological treasures, including gold artifacts or gold in any form. The search was conducted by the Gaddis Mining Company. (The company ceased operations when the government refused to allow it additional time) . . .

In March 1974, the Secretary of the Army granted entry under terms of a license issued to claimants who purport to know where the gold is located and seek only the opportunity to locate and remove it . . .

During the early part of August 1974, the State of New Mexico filed a suit . . . to enjoin the Army and any other group other than the State of New Mexico from searching for the treasure. The State contended that the State has an ownership interest in the treasure since it allegedly is located on State land leased to the Army . . .

On 22 August 1974, in denying the State's application for a temporary injunction against the Army, Judge Bratton in effect ordered the Army to permit no one to look for the lost treasure unless with the consent of both the State of New Mexico and the Army . . .

In view of these developments, the Army considers the treasure search matter closed for the time being. However, at such time as we are free once again to consider issuing permits to persons desiring to search for the alleged treasure, we will give full consideration to qualified individuals.

The Museum is the key

At this stage the outlook for entry was not encouraging.

The Department of Defense appeared to be talking out of both sides of its mouth: Eager to help, yet stipulating hard conditions as prerequisites to entry.

The outcome of other events foreshadowed more delay. Ova Noss' billion-dollar lawsuit was dismissed by the court upon motion of the Army, a result not particularly distressing to us, as the action was instituted more to impede the Bailey group's movement than obtain a hearing on the merits of her complaint.

While Norvell's litigation had accomplished something — requiring the concurrent consent of both state and federal governments — it did not relax the Army's ban on further exploration or recovery operations.

More significantly, Secretary of the Army Callaway had turned a deaf ear to the combined request of three New Mexico officials, Gov. Bruce King, Attorney General Norvell and Land Commissioner Alex Armijo. They wanted to see the Bailey group on the Missile Range first, to recover "a portion of the fabled Victoria Peak treasure."

In a telegram to Callaway, they said they would take no more than four persons and would remain on the premises no longer than 48 hours . . . . . Also, they would supply the necessary equipment for removal (of the gold). "It would be our intention to place the gold with the appropriate authority, federal or state, to hold in safekeeping until rights of various parties are determined by appropriate legal actions. It should be noted that this request does not affirm a belief by state officials that the gold is in fact present on or near this site. Rather it is designed to hopefully settle once and for all the specific allegations of the existence of the gold. This is a matter of extreme urgency."

By now it was even more firmly fixed in our minds that a plan of entry must be perceived by the Army to be fair and equitable. What that would entail, no one was quite certain.

Few persons had a better perception of the Army's dilemma than Norman Scott of Expeditions Unlimited, the Florida company specializing in retrieving valuable cargoes from sunken ships. For quite some time Scott had been active in the Noss case, shuttling with much secrecy between academic and government offices. His approach was both practical and logical: Let an organization like Expeditions Unlimited plan and carry out the project under sponsorship of a university, with claimants on the scene as observers. Obviously, Scott had taken a page out of the museum-sponsored, Gaddis company experience of a decade earlier.

Our last contact with Scott had taken place in Clovis two years earlier, when he tried without success to negotiate an agreement with the Noss family. As it happened, his visit to Clovis was on the day of John Dean's Watergate TV testimony about F. Lee Bailey and the excitement of that revelation summarily pushed Scott's offer to the back burner.

However, the turndown from us did not lessen Scott's appetite for the hunt, a reaction totally in keeping with his personality. A deep-chested man with a strident voice and keen eye he possessed an extraordinary zest for challenge — a predictable trait in one who made a living searching for treasures in ships long lost at sea. Accordingly, E. U.'s reputation as one of the few successful marine archeological firms was largely a testament to Scott's personal dynamism.

In June of '75 he had written to Secretary Callaway expressing his approval of the Army proposal, namely, a sequential entry, with the drawing of lots to determine which claimant would enter first. It was, I think, merely a gesture to get Callaway's attention and hopefully put Expeditions Unlimited on the Secretary's "active" list.

By late August Scott was in pursuit of reactions to his proposal for a scientific exploration of Victoria Peak. In a letter to Oscar Jordan of the Land Office, he urged the State of New Mexico to ask the Army to allow "a sophisticated scientific search of the adjacent Geronimo and Victoria Peak areas." Its purpose: "Determine the voids and the presence of dense material (if any) contained therein."

He named two companies with the equipment and know-how to conduct the probe — Stanford University Research Institute and Texas Instruments. Further, Expeditions Unlimited would be responsible for funding the project, and only claimants approved by the U. S. Army would be permitted onto the site to observe the activity.

He suggested the State of New Mexico Museum as sponsor in order "to protect all archeological treasures that may be found in the search . . . . . We contemplate that this initial search would not involve any recovery but merely to determine the presence of alleged material (gold)."

Then Scott's letter went on to state: "Please keep in mind that the Gaddis Mining Company spent large sums of money to no avail. Hopefully, today we have more sophisticated instrumentation . . . . . If these tests are in the negative, this is not necessarily conclusive. Conversely, if they are in the positive, they are quite conclusive!

"I have been advised by Mr. Bland West that he

would recommend our type of approach favorably to the Secretary of the Army."

Some of the pieces of Scott's plan fell into place immediately.

The Commissioner of Public Lands, Phil R. Lucero, said he would approve the scientific search. Director George H. Ewing of the New Mexico museum indicated the museum would participate in monitoring the field study.

The major roadblock was still the Army, as immovable as the Himalayas. Several strategies were tried, including outright appeals to sentiment in the effort to dissolve the impasse.

In one instance someone prevailed upon William F. Gorog, Board Chairman of Mead Technological Laboratories, to discuss the Army's ban with Callaway. Gorog was a good friend of Callaway's.

Callaway's response to Gorog was intended to put the situation in perspective. He told Gorog no one could be allowed on the Missile Range because of Judge Bratton's prohibition in the Norvell case.

Obviously, Callaway was in error; there was no such prohibition in the court's ruling. Bratton did rule, however, that the consent of both the state and the U. S. would be required for entry, and, further, gave to the Commander of White Sands the right to reject any plan that preferred one claimant over another.

Then, mere chance produced a development favorable to the claimants. Norman Scott somehow obtained a copy of Callaway's letter to Gorog. Detecting the error in Callaway's interpretation of the Bratton ruling, Scott dispatched lengthy letters both to Gorog and Bland West, pleading his case with luminous fervor and holding forth the prospect that his plan would solve the treasure trove riddle once and for all.

To the Army, that was a most attractive prospect. Another startling aspect came to the surface: The White

House had been informed of the Noss discovery in a 2 ½-page fact sheet prepared by the Army. It reviewed the history of the treasure trove, stated Noss "allegedly discovered a tunnel into Victoria Peak which led to a vast cavern 300 feet below ground containing stacks of gold bars, a gold crown, remnants of Wells Fargo chests and 27 skeletons chained to posts. As to the amount of this store of gold, a figure of 37 tons is often related. A former wife of Noss, Mrs. Ova Noss, in 1949 estimated the value of the gold at $350,000,000. Noss is said to have removed some 261 bars of gold each weighing 60 pounds, a crown and a statue of the Virgin Mary from the cavern."

The Scott plan impressed Callaway, particularly its suggestion on how to achieve an even-handed treatment of the claimants. Scott had zeroed in on the aspect with the greatest appeal to the Army, a way to settle the whole business of the treasure trove, perhaps forever. He underscored what the Army feared, that the demands of claimants would grow in number and fervor. Already, amidst the hue and cry, inquiries were beginning to come in from congressmen responding to pressure from the more influential, like Bailey and Scott. I myself contacted Senators Stuart Symington and Thomas Eagleton; both directed letters to the Department of the Army, asking for reviews of the Noss situation. Congressman McMahon made a similar appeal at Roscoe Parr's request.

Caught in a crossfire, the Army decided to give serious consideration to Norman Scott's plan and instructed Bland West to follow up as intermediary and planner.

The scientific scan of Victoria Peak and perhaps other areas would, under the Scott proposal, exclude all exploration. No digging or poking about for treasure, only a scan to locate large voids, such as caverns or caves, under the slopes of the peak. Should any be detected, another separate plan of entry would be decided upon and put into effect at a later date.

The electronic survey suggested by Scott was the one method certain to be opposed by the Parr and Bailey groups.

Parr's position had not changed; he had those personal instructions from Doc Noss which he was certain would lead him to a cache of gold bars.

Bailey's clients, on the other hand, needed no fancy detection equipment; they were presumed to know the exact location of a huge gold cache.

So, facing this almost certain opposition, the Army cautioned Scott that he must obtain the cooperation of all the claimants and satisfy them as to whatever plan was ultimately chosen.

By the summer of '76 there appeared to be excellent progress. Several claimants, including Ova Noss, had given oral and written approval of the Scott plan. Bailey was slow to commit his people but it was felt he would ultimately agree. Roscoe Parr remained adamantly opposed.

Oscar Jordan of the Land Office began circulating rough drafts of a treasure trove easement form which the State would use in the process of granting entry to Expeditions Unlimited and authorized representatives of each claimant.

Then came a rather weird turn of events, revealed in a memorandum prepared by Oscar Jordan of the State Land Office:

March 19, 1976
State Land Office

Norman Scott and Sam Scott initiated a confer-ence call this morning .... Sam reported that he had just talked to Shriver, one of the claimants, who has returned from England and is in Florida, and was advised that eleven tons of gold went out of White Sands Missile Range on March 10, 1976, by TWA Swiss Air to Credit Swiss in Zurich, Switzer-

land; that it cleared in Zurich on 3-10-76, shipped apparently out of Albuquerque International Airport, possibly through Chicago.

They discussed whether a lawsuit should be filed. I suggested they should first bring Shriver to New Mexico and talk to either the U. S. Attorney or Judge Bratton . . . . . That perhaps then they could get an investigation by the federal government which could go international and check out the shipments to Zurich.

4:00 p.m., same day:

Norman Scott called from Pompano Beach, Florida . . . . He said he personally talked to Shriver and that Shriver assures him that he has a witness who . . . . will furnish the names, dates and places pertaining to the removal of the shipment; that if he is given immunity from criminal prosecution, he will so testify. I suggested that Scott contact their attorney and have him contact the U. S. Attorney in Albuquerque to secure the immunity.

> *Oscar Jordan*
> *Legal Department*

Jordan's memo of the above conversations was placed in Land Office files.

Needless to say, the rumor of a movement of tons of gold out of the Missile Range drew wild reactions, none more bizarre than the speculation that the Bailey group had grown weary of the bickering and had engineered removal of the treasure. Similar unfounded suspicions were cast in the direction of the Parr group. An unidentified caller gravely suggested we check on the movements of Ova Noss over the past forty-eight hours.

The Scotts did not pursue the matter and, frustratingly, no one in position of authority made any further moves. Ultimately the matter was consigned to the company of fallacies that cling like barnacles to every lost-gold mystery.

It was tempting to reflect on the possibilities — first the digging, then the recovery of the gold, then the shipment to Switzerland. But other circumstances seemed to make that scenario a little too pat to be credible.

However, consider the following paragraphs which I dictated to my Noss file a year after the alleged Swiss shipment:

March 31, 1977

Received telephone call at home last night from a person who did not give his name but who said his father was a retired military man who worked in the security force at the White Sands Missile Range in the late '50's.

He said his father supervised the security operations that were involved in the removal of gold from the Noss cave by military personnel. He said that all of the gold was taken out at that time ...

The caller said the gold was all gone. The military got it.

He sounded most believable. I asked him to invite his father to call me and that I would preserve his anonymity. He called back to say his father was afraid to become involved at all, inasmuch as he is on pension and feared reprisals from the Army.

In this period F. Lee Bailey was engaged by the Hearst family to handle the defense of daughter Patty in her West Coast trial. Consequently, his involvement with the Noss matter was now sharply reduced. He engaged George T. Harris, Jr., an Albuquerque attorney, to share day-to-day details with Al Johnson, a Bailey associate.

Also at this time we observed a new surge of activity on the part of Joe Newman of El Paso, Texas. While he maintained a lively interest in all the developments, he was not inclined to discuss the basis of his claim or its origin. He had disclosed to close friends that he explored the Victoria Peak area in the early 70's with three or four friends when their presence was detected by military personnel. His companions were arrested, later released. Newman himself hid in a huge crevice and escaped notice.

By this time my own associates, Bob Martin and George O'Laughlin, had shed all semblance of curiosity in the Noss matter. What attention they did devote to it was confined to occasional attacks upon my sanity for continued involvement.

Despite the chiding, there was no reason for me to keep a wounded tongue in cheek. I knew Ova's predicament. Living from day to day, with the modest help she might expect from her family and others interested in the treasure trove, she was ever on the alert for ways to replenish a scant purse. The most frequent opportunities and - amazingly - the most productive were created by circumstances related to her ex-husband's discovery. It was to that well that she went frequently. A few dollars here and there helped her survive as she dreamed of the fabulous fortune that sooner or later, she was convinced, would be hers.

One evening in her trailer in Clovis we were discussing various provisions of the Scott proposal. Her mood was reflective as aspects of her life with Doc came to mind. She said she did not like the things they said about Doc in the Ryan trial, "calling him a drunk and a trouble-maker."

"One thing, though," she mused, "he was sure jealous about that gold. Oh, he'd let us see a bar now and then but he sure always took 'em away and hid 'em."

I asked, "Ova, tell me, how many bars of gold did you actually see in all the time Doc was out there on Victoria Peak?"

"Hundreds, and each one almost as big as a house brick."

"Yet he never gave you even a single bar, just for you to have, perhaps as a keepsake?"

She hesitated, as if trying to determine how best to explain a sensitive situation.

"He didn't let anybody see what he was doing when he was moving the gold out before the explosion." Then with a wry smile, "I think I could find a few bars if those dern government folks would let me go out there."

I never felt her memory, even in the face of her 79 years, was playing tricks on her.

Once during a visit in her trailer she produced a sword and a circlet of sterling silver, both of seeming ancient origin. She said she could show more items that came from the treasure rooms and might do so later. While I was inspecting the markings on the sword a son entered the trailer and sharply reprimanded her for letting anyone see it.

Members of her family betrayed a sense of real apprehension when she would recount events of the early years, as if fearing she might disclose some vital secret. Often they would interrupt her with a reproving remark — "Stop, don't tell that!" or "Momma, you've gone far enough."

On more than one occasion I chided her over the fact she had not produced a single bar of gold or a piece of one, if for no other reason than to strengthen our belief in her cause. She would shake her head; she had nothing to show.

But there is one "outsider" for whom she did produce a bar of ancient vintage — Howard Bryan, the esteemed columnist of the Albuquerque Tribune.

In the course of a visit with Ova in her trailer in Clovis, she showed him a gold bar. Its markings were an obvious clue to its origin.

She turned to him, her eyes hard as flint.

"This is what I have been trying to get my hands on all these years. Damn Army's probably stole all of it by now. Digging it out and hauling it off, the sons-of-bitches."

The deposition

Only two persons, Doc and Ova, knew the full story of what really took place that fall day on Victoria Peak and only Ova was left to tell it. So, counsel felt it was time for her to give a full accounting in a dependable situation — *under oath* in a judicial proceeding. Apart from the logic of recording her own story in such circumstances, one had to recognize the reality of age; she was nearing her eightieth birthday.

There was still another reason why a formal telling was crucial. Her eyewitness account of Doc's movements at the Peak would simplify the issue of ownership — now a tangled web of opposing claims. And help to determine whether in point of law he was the sole owner of the gold. If so, the claims of subsequent finders would be adversely affected.

The opportunity for Ova's deposition came sooner than expected, conveniently in connection with her lawsuit against the State of New Mexico and Bailey's unnamed clients.

A number of attorneys assembled in the offices of an Albuquerque law firm on March 24, 1975, some representing clients named in Ova's petition, others with only an indirect interest. But all admittedly excited over the prospect of hearing the story of the treasure trove told under oath for the first time by a participant.

Among those present:

George T. Harris for the F. Lee Bailey group.

Scott McCarty for Violet Yancy.

Jay Knight for the Shriver group.

Mrs. Letha Guthrie, Mrs. Noss' daughter.

No one appeared for the State of New Mexico.

In preliminary questioning, counsel sought to impress upon Ova the importance of giving "careful, thoughtful, honest answers to the best of your ability."

The questioning led her into a review of the early years of her life: Her birth in Saffordville, Kansas. Her four children by an early marriage. Her surviving sister and two brothers. The movements of the family to Texas, Oklahoma, and New Mexico. Her own travels as a piano player and teacher. Her marriage to Milton Ernest (Doc) Noss at Sayre, Oklahoma, in the fall of '31.

She said she knew little about Doc's family, except that he had one sister, no longer living, that his practice as a "licensed" foot doctor was in an office on Polk street in Hot Springs (Truth or Consequences), N.M.

The first she knew "Doc had discovered something", she said, was in the fall of 1937 when they and two other couples were on a deer hunt in the Victoria Peak area. The men had returned toward dusk but Noss was not with them. They said they had lost track of him several hours before and were worried, fearing he might have fallen into a mountain crevice and hurt himself. While the evening meal was in progress Ova saw Doc approaching at a distance and rushed to meet him.

He told her, "Get your work done early and come to bed. I've got something to tell you."

"What did he tell you?"

"All he knew at that time was that he'd found old workings of some kind."

Two weeks passed, she said, before they returned to the site. Doc had bought a bread wagon to haul a few pieces of equipment. They went to a spot east of the hunting camp, then trudged to the top of Victoria Peak.

"What was it that you saw that very first time?"

"We found an overhanging ledge and a room beneath. There's two points on Victoria Peak. We was on the highest point."

"Did anyone know the two of you had come to the area?"

"No."

"And what was it that you saw there?"

"I saw three, well, four walls. There was this overhanging shelf that hung over as a sort of roof and protected a deep ledge."

She said the ledge was about twenty feet below the overhang, maybe more. She and Doc picked their way down to the ledge and found themselves in a space that appeared to have been used as living quarters. "We couldn't see what their idea was in making a kind of home there. And then we noticed over in the south wall, right in a corner, a large flat rock. It had a rat's nest built over it, being there a long time. So, we brushed that off and there was this thick rock and we pried it up and pushed it to one side and air come right up in our face like that, like opening up a vent in your air conditioner and dirt blows out."

She said the rock was about two or three inches thick and "it fit over this hole, just about even with it, twenty-four inches wide and forty-two long.

Q. Did it look like a natural rock?

A. No. It had little breakings, like it had been chiseled out. We figured it had been there a long, long time, but we could not figure the age of it.

Q. After you pried the lid up, what next?

A. We seen a ladder in a crevice. It had two poles and came up like that (indicating). Each step was niched and tied with straps of leather. Maybe they was secure once but now so old that on the second step down, one broke, and Doc fell about eight inches until he hit the next step, so we had to work and maneuver to remove that ladder. The wood itself was so brittle it would snap if you stepped on it, so that made us believe it had been there a long time.

Doc spent the following weekend checking the deep crevice and testing the safety of indentations in the crevice walls. They gave him a footing to a depth of only about 40 feet into the almost vertical shaft.

Ova said he used a 45-foot lariat rope to measure the distance and went as far as the rope would let him go. "Finally we come up with five lariat ropes and tied them, one to another. That let him down eventually but he didn't do it in one trip. He was afraid; he had to feel his way and it was as dark as a dungeon down there.

"We had a 2-cell flashlight but it wasn't big enough. Then we brought one that would shoot a 1,500-foot beam, penetrate real deep. I've still got it. The thing is that long (indicating)."

As the weeks and months passed, Noss worked his way deeper into the shaft, attempting only a few yards in each descent, for the return to the top was always physically exhausting and dangerous.

"He had a Brunton compass and a Lufkin tapeline. They're the accurate instruments of measurements and directions. He went down as far as thirty-eight feet, and held the flashlight while he went down. He had tied a knot in this lariat rope every two feet so he could have a grip and wouldn't slip or fall and could hug his feet around the other knots.

"It was in the spring of '38 before he reached a landing. He knew he was facing north. He had his instruments and his back was to the south. Directly to his left, there was five boulders that went down into a tunnel. And then there would be sickly fumes coming up there, and engineers have told us that it was volcanic ash. We didn't know what the fumes were, but his legs would break out around the top of his socks, so there was something that was alkali in there that would break his legs out. And so, he didn't venture down that way and he went directly to his left, down a path, downhill, sort of downhill."

Q. Now, you have told us something about paintings on the wall. Where were these paintings that you're talking about?

A. In the thirty-eight foot ledge where it was we got in.

Q. And what kind of paintings were those?

A. Mummified figures with two legs and things like that on them, and maybe trees and a horse and a man on a horse, an Indian, or something like that, you know. They were man-made.

Ova said the farthest she had gone down into the shaft was some 118 feet. Later, daughter Letha was allowed to descend to a somewhat deeper level.

Q. What role did you play in assisting Doc as he explored the shaft?

A. Well, he told me the mountain was rotten. If his foot kicked a rock loose, there might be tons of earth roll down on him, so we had a clothes-line rope we called a tug rope. We had signals; two tugs meant something and three tugs meant something else. And then we had a rope, a one-and-five-eights-inch manila rope for him to climb in and out with.

Q. On the occasions when Doc would go down into the hole, could you see him?

A. Oh, I could see him to a great distance, until he hit a spiral. When he went down in that spiral, I lost sight of him, except that his flashlight would flash up and I could see the reflections, but I couldn't see his body.

Q. How long was it before there came a time when something came out of that hole that you or he thought was of value?

A. March or April of '38. About six months. He brought out different things.

Q. Now, from November, '37, when he first discov-

183

ered there was something at Victoria Peak, to the time when he first brought something out of the hole, six months later, was anyone there other than you and Doc?

A. No, just us.

Q. Had your children gone there?

A. No. We had told them about it, though.

Q. Well, will you describe the occasion when he first brought something out of the hole?

A. First he had a packsaddle made, just like a vest. A big pocket in front and a pocket in the back, and it buckled right around so he could keep his hands free and put articles in the pockets, you know.

Q. And when he came out of the opening what did he have with him that he did not have when he went into it?

A. He had a lot of money, a lot of loose money. He had come upon the morrals, a leather thing that they put feed in and strap around the horse's head. And these morrals were full of money, but they were rotten. He went to lift them up and the bottom fell out and money went everywhere in the dirt and dust.

Q. He brought money out?

A. Oh, yes, he had his pockets full. He didn't have this jacket then that I'm speaking about. He had his pockets full, and a bank sack that he took down with him.

Q. You said money. Anything else at that time?

A. No, but he told me about lots of jewels.

Q. Will you describe what the money looked like?

A. Well, all of it was old foreign money; very little of it American money. I got one and I still have it, an English half crown, 1803.

Q. Now, you had a conversation with him about what else was down there.

A. Yes, he said there was lots of crowns. He said there

were trunks and clothing, and he seen lots of chains with crosses on them, lots of jewels. There was evidently a chest that had a lid that would come open. I never questioned him about it, but he could raise that lid up and see in there, and there was quite a bag of stuff in there. And he told me that there must have been the biggest market the world ever seen in pig iron. He said he never seen such ricks. He told me how long he thought they were, double ricks.

She said the descent into the treasure rooms and the climb back were so difficult he could make only a single trip on any given weekend. She said he always brought a pocket or two full of coins and jewels — "Oh, there was a lot of money down there!"

Q. Can you describe to us the jewels that he brought out?

A. They were some jewels, not in the rough but I mean unset.

Q. Okay. Did there come a time when he brought out any of this metal that he talked about, that was pig iron?

A. He brought out one bar. It was in April of '38.

Q. Who was present?

A. Just him and I. He was down there more than four hours and I was worried because there had been no tug on the rope, and he finally tugged the rope. And I had lunch fixed and coffee, and he hollered, "I'm a-coming up."

Q. What did he have with him?

A. He pulled a brick out and tossed it out on the ground; it just kind of scooted. He said that was the last one of these things he'd ever bring out. He pretty near tossed it down two or three times because it was so heavy, but he brought it up to let me see it. It looked kind of tarnished and the sun was high and I was sitting here and him over there and the metal was over here (indicating). And I looked at it and it didn't interest me and we ate. And finally I went over there and started to pick it up. I couldn't it was so heavy. So, he handed me his knife and I put it under it and I rolled it over, but when I did, why, it had scuffed on them pebbles and it was shiny. And I said, "Look here, Doc, that's yellow." And he come over, his legs still a-shaking and trembling from straining in coming out, and he took his knife and he scraped that bar and —

Q. Go ahead, what did he say?

A. Well, he had a shocked look and he said, "This is gold! This is gold!"

Q. Now, what else did he say?

A. He said the bars were stuck down in the caverns, and the ribbing come up against the wall, like this is the wall (indicating), and this ribbing come up, and there was dirt from here right over to the edge. He raked off the dirt and the bars were a-laying there, stuck together, and he used his knife to pop one loose.

Q. Describe the bar that you yourself saw on that first occasion. What size was it?

A. I would say about twelve to fifteen inches long, and four-and-a-half or five inches wide, about two inches thick.

Q. I take it that was not the only one he brought out?

A. Oh, no, not when he had seen all that. He could hardly — he closed his office and we would head back on Thursday and be there Friday, Saturday and Sunday.

Q. And when you went back the next time what did you do?

A. He went down the shaft and he was there a long time. He carried — he had to take his food down there, for he knew he was going to be there a long time. And when he come back out he handed me a letter that he had in his pocket. He said, "Here, put this in your purse." I said, "Where is the envelope?" He said, "Let me tell you something. I left it under a bar, I propped it there, and if anybody tries to beat me out of it, they know very good and well they're a thief."

Q. And what did he tell you on that occasion about how many bars there were down there?

A. He said there was so many long and so many high, stacked like cordwood, and double ricks. He figured it up and it came to more than 16,000 bars. And then there was more over in another rick. Doc made visits to the treasure rooms on a regular basis. Later, he closed his office permanently. We couldn't close it immediately because he didn't know how to make any money. It took money to keep us operating. The law was, then, in those days it was illegal to own gold forty-eight hours without turning it in. He was under a lot of pressure.

Q. Could you tell us what you saw with your own eyes, how many bars actually were taken out of the hole by Doc Noss in your presence?

A. I helped him with eighty-six bars.

Q. Any others?

A. I saw about twenty he brought in and laid on the kitchen table.

Q. To your knowledge, any others?

A. He took, I think, practically all that was stamped — that we knew was pure.

Q. Have you any idea of the total number of bars that Doc Noss may have taken out?

A. Several hundred. He worked at night, sometimes all day —

Q. Did he always work in your presence?

A. Yes, except at night, and then I would go up on top and sleep in a bedroll while he was down there working. He would come up the next morning and sweat would be all through his khaki clothes, and he would sleep practically all day he was so tired.

Q. So, then, you do not, of your own knowledge, know the total number of bars he may have removed?

A. No, I don't know the total number. But I know there was a lot of them, for he knew the wealth that was down there. I've seen close to 150 to 200 on different occasions.

She said her daughter Letha came to the peak for the first time late that summer and stayed with Ova in a motel room in Las Cruces. They moved from Hot Springs because "we were getting too many jibes from people who knew we had got it and wanted to get their foot in." Word of the discovery spread rapidly after Doc had taken one of the bars to a gold buyer. His eyes wide with amazement, the buyer asked where it was found, explaining that some prospectors were looking for gold in the Caballos mountains. Was it there that Doc had found the bar? Ova related that Doc just grinned and let the man think his gold had come from the Caballos, which are southwest of the San Andres and Victoria Peak.

Q. As a result of that visit did anything happen out in the Caballos at that time?

A. Oh, yes. The buyer said he wasn't going to tell anybody but by Monday morning the Caballos looked like Chinatown, tents everywhere. Oh, they were thick — and we had to show up at the Caballos or they would know where we was going. So, it was hunt the button, I'm telling you. It was quite a game.

Q. What did Doc do?

A. He moved some bars from the San Andres over to the Caballos to get the people out of his hair. He acted as if he had discovered the bars there, four or five bars, and he let them see the bars. We went back to the San Andres where we knew they would leave us alone.

Even with all that gold they knew there were certain problems. More than anything else, she said, they feared an investigation by the FBI. They resisted the temptation to possess the gold physically, thinking that by hiding it they would not be deemed guilty of possession.

She said, "We couldn't live good. We had to work. Once somebody put a kidnapping note on our door and a jewelerman came one night at the back door and he said, 'You better get out of town. They're going to kidnap you.' We left and went to Gallup, New Mexico."

What did Doc do with the gold that he brought out those first few times?

"He hid it in various spots, because we knew that eventually the Missile Range was coming in there, and he had to get it off of the property."

"And did you personally hide any bars yourself?"

"I went with him when he hid twenty-six, and I believe they're undisturbed today. I think I'm the only person knows where to go."

She said they knew for sure in March it was gold, when they submitted one for assay to a Jimmy Gantz in El Paso and later to an assaying firm, Holly and Holly, in Douglas, Arizona. Later she checked the firm's records, in 1949, and verified the Holly and Holly assay.

Not long after his discovery, she said, Doc hired a young man named Serafin Sedillo, who went down with him to the treasure rooms "to help carry it out." Sedillo worked only a few weeks.

She described a thick sharp rock that protruded into the shaft and at times would sever the rope used by Doc to descend into the shaft below the overhanging ledge. Doc decided to enlarge it, so he hired a dynamite expert named C. E. Montgomery to blast open a larger space.

"Montgomery overloaded it with dynamite and ruined everything," Ova said. "Rocks went fifty feet up in the air and rolled down the canyon, and dust like to never settled. Why, Doc chased him off the peak right then and there."

Q. What did you see at the top after the explosion?

A. It was a pile of rubble deep down into the shaft. It was a mess. I don't know how to tell you. Everything had to be done over and a new shaft worked down there. The large room where the paintings were, it shattered the walls and everything. It was all filled in. Debris had to be all pulled out of there.

Q. Did you sink a shaft where the room had originally been?

A. Yes. It's there intact today.

Q. And describe that shaft that you dug.

A. Four by five feet, and it hung on collars on top of the earth, collars of big timbers. And we had bolts several feet long that went into these four by fives, each one, everything just swinging on these two collars that lay on top of the mountain.

Q. Who sunk the shaft?

A. Claude Fincher, an old retired carpenter, and Doc.

Q. How deep did it go?

A. Thirty-eight feet.

Q. Did the thirty-eight feet take you down below the original floor of the large room?

A. No. It took us to where the original rock place was laying.

Q. Okay. So, the shaft took you down to where you had originally found the plate?

A. Yes.

Q. So, in other words, this explosion had just about completely filled in the natural room where the paintings were.

A. Yes, that's right. But the shaft filled up a lot deeper, maybe about 120 feet down.

She paused for a moment. "He put eighty sticks in

there, I think."

"Eighty sticks of what?"

"Dynamite."

"So, when you dug your shaft down to that place where the plate was, did you then have to continue digging beyond that, down into the hole?"

"Oh, yes."

"And how many people helped you at that point, to try and open up the shaft?"

"Oh, Doc had a lot of people hired then. He had to have help. We built a windlass. Do you know what they are? It had a bucket about so big, but awful deep, and they let it down and filled it up. And then they turned a crank and windlassed it up to the top and dumped it."

At one time, she said, there were thirty workers at the peak for a period of six months.

"So, you're telling us in effect that you tried for a year to clean the shaft?"

"Yes, it was a mess. We had no money and, well, they called us the Hardly Able Mining Company. That's because we had a mess."

"How could you afford to run thirty men at a time? Were these people working for nothing?"

"Some was so interested that they preferred to get their clothes and their board and a small interest, and others wanted pay."

She was asked whether the name Sonny or Joe Andregg was familiar to her.

"Yes, sir, he was one of Doc's trusted help. He was there in '40."

"What kind of work did Andregg actually do?"

"They would go out with horses, one for Doc and one for him, and sometimes two lead horses. And they was carrying gold bars."

"You saw with your own eyes Sonny Andregg and Doc Noss moving gold bars?"

"Yes. When Doc give up with the explosion and

couldn't dig down any further, he began getting busy and moving the stuff."

She said that for reasons of safety he hid the bars in numerous places.

Q. Numerous places?

A. Yes, if he put his eggs all in one basket, if they found the place, they would find it all.

Q. What did you see, if anything, that supports your understanding that Doc hid gold bars in a number of places?

A. I seen the horses go out weighted down. I seen them come back empty.

Q. Will you tell us what Doc did, if anything, to try and turn gold into cash?

A. Well, he sold some for $20.67 an ounce at the Texas border in Mexico at various times when we would get short of money. Took a great loss on it.

Q. Let me ask you this: Did you ever see gold nuggets that Doc had made?

A. Yes. He went to El Paso with gold bars, and the man there had a board about this long and about this wide (indicating) with deep, scooped-out places. And this man would put a fire to the gold and put white fluxing or something on there. I don't know what that was for. But anyway, it was a solidified thing. And it cooled a little and he would drop it right over in, with tweezers, over into the vat. And he made barrels, maybe not barrels of nuggets, but he made me a lot of them.

Q. So Doc took gold bullion and converted it into nuggets form.

A. He gave them to me and that was my means of buying food for the workers out there.

She was asked about someone who was a buyer of old gold in Phoenix, Ariz. She replied, "Yes, his shop was right across from the Adams Hotel. We took two bars to the shop and he bought them. He came by and showed us a check for $32,000. He called the bank and said the bank had confirmed his check was good. Doc got over to the bank and they said, 'We're sorry, Doc, but the buyer called in and stopped payment on the check.' And Doc said, 'Oh!' He had left his gold up there in his office. He hurried right back and the buyer had locked his door and gone, and we were out our two bars of gold."

"Were there other times when you sold gold?"

"Doc took five bars to the Denver Mint in '41 or '42. He thought if he couldn't deal with people he would go to the government. I was in the car. Claude Fincher and Doc carried it into the mint. The mint people were going to confiscate it. They said it was old gold and accused him of stealing it in Mexico. They gave him a hold certificate or receipt for the $97,000 worth of gold bars."

"Now, was there a time when Doc was going to sell a large quantity of gold?"

"Fifty-one bars."

"And when was that?"

"In 1949, in February."

"Who was he going to sell them to?"

"To Charlie Ryan. He owned the Ryan Tool Company in Alice, Texas."

She said the deal with Ryan called for an airplane, rented by Ryan, to land in Hembrillo basin and fly the gold to an unspecified destination. A bulldozer had scraped out a clearing wide enough for a landing "right out over the saddle near the mountain range, about five miles from Victoria Peak."

Q. Now, at or about the time when he was making this sale, was there an airplane crash near Victoria Peak, not involving the Ryan plane?

A. Yes. We had a bulldozer down in our canyon, clearing a hairpin road to Victoria Peak, and the operator broke a part that swings the blade, so my son Marvin went to Hot Springs to get another part. It wasn't a big enough town, so he went to

El Paso to get it. He picked up a friend of his there who piloted a small plane. He was the brother of the guy who was running the bulldozer. Near Victoria Peak they had a downdraft and the plane nosed down, came down flat and busted. Well, it killed the pilot outright. And Marvin was injured pretty bad. His back broke and his leg broke in a lot of places, and the stick rammed up into his groin. They took him to the hospital down in El Paso.

Q. Now, how long before Doc's death was this?

A. The day before.

Q. Did Doc help get Marvin to the hospital?

A. He carried him. He literally picked him up and grabbed a mattress and carried him, rode with him all the way down there.

When he returned from the hospital, he told Ova that he had changed his mind about going through with the deal with Ryan Tool.

She said the reason was that Ryan didn't have the money with him. "He was going to take the gold and pay Doc after he had transported it. It was no deal. No money, no gold."

"So, as far as you knew, Doc went off to move gold?"

"He did. I know, I have proof of that."

"He went off to move gold and you went on to see Marvin at the hospital?"

"Yes."

"What's the next time you saw Doc?"

"Dead."

"What were the circumstances of his death?"

"It's come out in court - what Ryan did, and all."

"Well, were you present in court?"

"You betcha, in the front row."

"Charles Ryan was tried in a local court here in New Mexico for the alleged killing of your husband?"

"He was tried in Las Cruces."

"So, at the time of Doc's death, the circumstances were that the mine shaft had not been completely cleared out?"

"No."

"And neither one of you had gained access again to the treasure?"

"No."

"Did you do any work after Doc died?"

"Well, yes, I sure did. I worked in '50 and '51, at Victoria Peak."

"What were you doing?"

"Trying to dig the shaft out with buckets. Thirty people volunteered to come in at different times, in relays. About nine or ten at a time."

"In 1951, what happened?"

"The Army made us move off. They gave us 2400 hours, or something, the way they time it. And I said, in my language, 'When does the time expire?' And they said, 'In two weeks.'"

Newsmen and crew at the '77 exploration.

"And when they told you to get off, did you voluntarily leave?"

"No. I made them move me off, because I thought I was big as they was."

"How did they do that, physically?"

"I waited to see. And they drove out there with a gun-carrier Jeep and waited behind until we left the canyon."

"So, when you left, you closed up the opening?"

"We sure did, and put a padlock on it."

Some of the equipment brought onto the Peak by Expeditions Unlimited.

"Operation Goldfinder"

Phil A. Koury, Esquire
10236 Bunker Ridge Road
Kansas City, Missouri 64137   17 June 1976

Dear Phil:

Confirming our recent telephone conversation, the Secretary of the Army has approved in concept the Norman Scott project to conduct some scientific testing at White Sands Missile Range to determine whether the conditions are such that the legendary lost treasure of Doc Noss might be located there in either section 16 or section 9. If Mrs. Noss wishes to be represented as an observer during the testing, in person or by an agent, please contact Colonel Tony Movsesian, Staff Judge Advocate at White Sands, to make appropriate arrangements. My latest information is that the testing is scheduled to go off between 6 and 14 July 1976.

Thank you for the memorandum from Oscar Jordan concerning the reported shipment of eleven tons of gold out of White Sands by TWA to Switzerland. I should not be surprised at weird reports like this, but I always am. I wonder if it will ever stop.

Best regards.

Sincerely,
Bland West

Deputy General Counsel
(Military and Civil Affairs)

The Norman Scott plan for entry into the Victoria Peak area appeared to be well on its way by mid-July of '76. Scott had entered his formal request to the Army for scientific studies. The tests would take about a week. He asked to be allowed to bring a team from the Stanford Research Institute onto WSMR for ground radar studies. As in the Gaddis exploration, the State of New Mexico Museum would act as project sponsor and monitor the probe in the event artifacts are uncovered.

In the meantime the Land Office in Santa Fe sent waiver documents to the claimants to qualify them as observers during Operation Goldfinder.

According to Lambert T. Dolphin, a senior physicist at the Stanford Institute, subsurface radar and sonic waves would probe the peak for hidden vaults and passageways. If something were found, Scott would then seek Army permission to place metal detectors and cameras within the peak. "If we locate a stock of gold bars, I guess we've got a pretty good case," he said.

Scott had informed the Army he would like to start the survey no later than June 15. Later the target date was changed to mid-July but more delays and complications were ahead.

On June 30 the Army command at White Sands announced the project was postponed at the request of Expeditions Unlimited and a new date would be set "sometime within the next sixty days." EU gave as the reason for the delay the illness of key technical operators of electronic equipment. There was a further delay when Stanford Research Institute asked for more time to allow subcontractors to calibrate and test instruments.

Six months passed with no firm date set. Then, without prior notice, Scott sent a new proposal to the Army. It drastically changed his original plan: "I see no sense in entering the base and probing only one site when our vast research investigations show that legitimate claims point to four specific locations."

What Scott was saying was that he now had confidence in locations other than the Noss mine, contending they too offered valid possibilities. "It serves no purpose whatsoever to go in and look at only one site. If we don't find the treasure, six months later another claimant will step forth and say, 'We should have looked over there.' Then, the Army is back in the same position." He also asked the White Sands command to let him bring onto the Missile Range a bulldozer and a front-end loader "to open up some known caves or shafts which allegedly lead to a treasure trove." He said they would search one area at a time. Two of the four areas would take possibly a day. The other two would take considerably more time.

Informed of the proposal, Ova Noss sent word to Scott he would be wasting his time if he went digging into places other than Victoria Peak. She would be at the site but, she advised bluntly, would not cooperate with the new plan.

The Bailey and Parr groups also said they would not take part in the project.

Bailey told newsmen he was seriously thinking of filing a lawsuit to halt the expedition unless each claimant filed a letter describing the exact location of the gold. Retorting, Scott accused Bailey of trying to force the other claimants into disclosing their secrets, while his own group refused to make such a disclosure or even reveal their identities.

In a letter to Secretary Callaway, Bailey replied Expeditions Unlimited was engaged in "simply a subterfuge for a program of prospecting and exploration made to solidify a claim which has no legal foundation."

As expected, Roscoe Parr informed the Land Office that he was "the only legitimate claimer" and that he alone should be permitted onto the range. In a letter to

Bland West he again revealed his deep resentment, condemning the Army for reversing what was heretofore a firm policy of refusing to allow any search whatever by persons without legitimate claims. He pressed the point he was in possession of instructions from Doc Noss on how to locate the treasure trove. He said he "only asked for a reasonable period of time to be able to make entry (into the treasure rooms) and carry out (Doc Noss') instructions." He said he has "conclusive evidence that there exists a cavern under some of the lands located on the White Sands Missile Range and is able to locate this cavern, as previously stated, without the assistance of electronic field surveys to be conducted by Expeditions Unlimited, Inc."

Parr's greatest fear centered on the Army's attitude should the exploration prove a failure. Would the Army then refuse to allow him to undertake a search based on Doc's instructions? The question was fair, and critical to Parr's position.

The Army was showing signs of becoming apoplectic over the bickering among the claimants, a real burr under its seat. It felt it had made its position abundantly clear. The ground rules were simple: Sophisticated equipment to determine the presence, if any, of large voids or caverns within Victoria Peak. If any voids were found, then a new arrangement for a later re-entry would have to be made with the Army in order to ascertain what, if anything, is contained in the voids. But there was no official assurance that a secondary exploration would be permitted.

At the twelfth hour Expeditions Unlimited was proposing a whole new program — use of heavy excavating equipment, adding new claimants and new locations.

Understandably, the Army's 5-page, single-spaced letter to EU president Scott was angry, sarcastic. Further, it made an astonishing charge against the claimants:

"The fact is that we never believed that any claimant knew or knows the locations of the legendary treasure. We recognize as qualified for a permit those claimants who told a plausible story concerning their knowledge of the treasure location. Another way of saying it is that the most convincing liars were recognized as qualified claimants, plus those who believed their gold fantasies."

That accusation was followed by one even more surprising. After reviewing what it felt was the status of the project at this point, the letter grew suddenly becalmed, almost philosophic.

"Upon further reflection we have just about concluded it might be to the Army's advantage to have you represent any and all persons who claim to know the location of the treasure or wish to be allowed to explore for it. The reason is obvious. If you are allowed to conduct a search for the treasure in one or more locations on WSMR and find only dry holes, as you almost certainly will, then the Army will be justified in refusing for the next decade or so to issue a treasure trove permit to anyone, on the grounds that the legend has been effectively debunked. Accordingly, as long as there is no indication of any treasure seeker with whom you contract taking advantage of the situation in order to promote a confidence game, we will no longer object to your representation of claimants heretofore unknown to the Army."

The roller coaster of changes, retreats and savage infighting came to a stop. Expeditions Unlimited was now in a position to proceed freely.

A new date for entry was agreed upon — March 19 to 28.

The Army's concession was not without limitations; EU could do only so much searching, probing and removing of gold within a 10-day period. Also, considering the mood of Army officials, Scott could not reasonably expect a grant of additional time.

It was now rumored the project was being financed by the millionaire Texan, Clint Murchison, who was said to own a substantial interest in EU. While refusing to comment on the Murchison relationship, Scott told us that he, Scott, had $80,000 to spend on the project. He also said his company has entered into an arrangement with Mrs. Violet Noss Yancy by which EU had received a percentage of her claim.

The name of another in the cast of Noss characters entered the picture at this point — Air Force Captain Leonard Fiege, whose whereabouts had remained something of a mystery following his separation from the service. Scott had not mentioned Fiege in his letters to the Army but later let it be known that it was Fiege who helped whet Scott's desire to explore locations other than the Noss claim, surely including the cavern entered by Fiege and a companion in 1958.

Army officials quickly called the attention of claimants to the dangers of the mission.

"The terrain is very rugged" their directives counseled, "and the temperature in that area can rise to as high as 120 degrees Fahrenheit during the day and below freezing at night."

They warned of natural desert hazards, including "poisonous snakes and scorpions, unexploded explosives both above and below the surface, unexpended projectiles, missile debris, dangerous tunnels."

As if these life threats were not enough, we were told to bring our own food, water and fuel, that we must leave the range before dark and suggested amicably that we make our own housing arrangements in local communities.

In a further flourish of civility, Col. Anthony A. Movsesian of the Staff Judge Advocate office added a few more stipulations:

Claimants may take turns observing the electronic survey on WSMR, but only one person from each claimant's group will be allowed to observe at a time.

Each person must remain with one of the working groups of Expeditions Unlimited, Inc., under escort. No straying from the group will be allowed.

The exact routes of entry and exit will be assigned by the project officer. Deviation from these routes will not be allowed.

No firearms or alcoholic beverages will be allowed within the license area.

Other than items which the person may bring into the license area, nothing will be removed from Sections 16 and 9.

Any violation will bar the offending individual from re-entry onto WSMR.

The figure at the upper right is Norman Scott, president of Expeditions Unlimited (supervisor of the '77 exploration), holding a morning press conference standing on the bed of a truck and speaking into a mike to a crowd composed largely of reporters and photographers.

The big search

Sitting stolidly in the center of Hembrillo basin, Victoria Peak appeared as forbidding as the treacherously uneven canyon floor. It was easy to see how its deep crevices, partly formed by earthen arms pointing skyward, might offer a safe refuge for contraband or treasure.

I remembered how amiable the peak appeared from a distance of several hundred yards on that day I watched the Gaddis exploration fourteen years ago. But now, standing at its base, I felt an inexplicable strength threatening to anyone tempted to probe its dark, plunging fissures.

The Scott expedition made its base camp at Radium Springs, twenty-five miles west of the search area, and early the morning of March 19, 1977, fifty vehicles traveled the fifteen miles to Hell Site, the Army's checkpoint. The passengers, almost a hundred, were then transferred to 4-wheel military jeeps. The journey of several miles over desert terrain to Victoria Peak was a body-throbbing experience. Our vehicle contained mostly Expeditions Unlimited personnel, excluding Norman Scott, who had been driven to the site earlier.

the first day ...

We see crews of Stanford Research Institute workmen setting scores of foot-high stakes at various points along the upper reaches of the western slope. The stakes are connected by a wire leading to radar scanning instruments.

Dressed in a purple pants suit, Ova Noss is settled in a jeep provided by the Army near the base of the peak. In her usual sprightly fashion she holds court for those eager to make her acquaintance or solicit her comment on the operations in progress.

At least fifty reporters and a score of photographers are on hand, some from major papers and news magazines, including *The New York Times, Time* and *Newsweek.* A television crew from CBS is filming what later would be a segment on "Sixty Minutes".

Museum of New Mexico personnel keep a close watch on all the activities in case anyone should uncover artifacts or ancient data with the slightest historical significance.

Norman Scott is the central figure. Accompanied by tanned, blond women assistants, he is in constant touch with his crew of workers, most of them divers more experienced at probing for treasures at sea than in subterranean chambers. He moves swiftly by jeep from one site to another as preparations for digging go forward in several locations at the same time.

the second day . . .

One might liken the occasion to a day at the county fair as the crowd separated in small groups and chatted. There is no way to observe the serious business of exploration in progress high up on the peak, much of it out of sight of the people below.

Sightseeing strolls in any direction are politely and firmly discouraged by the military . . . . . stern warnings about snakes and unexploded missiles.

Unless known on sight, one can only guess as to which of the six claimants are present. F. Lee Bailey is not here, nor his associate Al Johnson. We hear E. D. Patterson, aligned with the Bailey group, is in the vicinity. Also Joe Newman. If William Shriver is on hand we did not learn of it.

Bailey's absence is puzzling, especially in light of his frequent challenge to state and federal officials that, given a few hours or less, certain clients of his could pinpoint the location of millions in gold bars. One might speculate that he wished to keep the location a secret in anticipation of a later solo effort at recovery. Or, protecting what he deemed his clients' best interests, he may have decided it is unwise to let anyone else recover "their" gold and subsequently see it forced into court on the issue of ownership.

Ova Noss is advised by counsel to offer only token cooperation with Scott in view of the fact he represents Ova's most serious competitor, Violet Noss Yancy. Ova openly criticizes the Scott program, insisting he is wasting valuable time probing for the gold in locations other than by way of Doc Noss' shaft at the top of Victoria Peak.

the third day . . .

There are no press or information handouts of any kind. It is virtually impossible to ascertain just exactly how the effort is progressing. The Army is tight-lipped. But occasionally Scott, like a latter day Moses, comes down from the mountain and gives reporters an opportunity to ask questions. His replies are cautious: Yes, the project is moving along. No, nothing of consequence to report. This morning, and each morning thereafter, he delivers a brief report from the bed of a truck, commenting on the prior day's activities.

This morning he announces they have found the so-called Dome Room by excavating a side entrance on Victoria Peak, the one believed to have been entered by Leonard Fiege in 1958. Then a surprise: Scott says Fiege himself helped workmen dig out the debris for nearly five hours, then entered the room only to find it contained nothing.

Later, Fiege tells reporters how he found stacks of

gold bars the last time he was in the cavern but "now it's entirely different. There are timbers in there now. It's all shored up."

One of the two workers who entered the room believes someone has done a lot of work in the cave, and adds, "There's even a campsite in there with a tea kettle, a No. 5 can that still has five sticks of dynamite and some old rotted fuse. There's even a pair of red corduroy pants."

the fourth day . . .

A backhoe is seen inching its way up the steep side of Victoria Peak to begin an attack on the collapsed shaft, dubbed "Chimney shaft", the one entered by Doc Noss in 1937 and which led him ultimately to the treasure rooms. The space where work in the shaft is to begin is only large enough to accommodate one man with a pick. No one believes they will be able to complete the job in the time remaining.

Excavation by others through the years has cleared out more than a hundred feet of Chimney shaft, now blocked by dirt and debris for a distance of 33 feet. Scott tells us that if this 33-foot "plug" can be removed his people would view the prospects as favorable. But they know that beyond the "plug" is a complicated series of passages and crevices — which means there would still be 2,000 feet between the searchers and the treasure rooms.

While activity at Chimney shaft is getting underway, a bulldozer moves toward Geronimo Peak, a mile to the north. There it will begin excavation at yet another site known as Bloody Hands, so-called because of five red handprints visible on a rock wall.

Still another key figure in the Noss story appears at the site — Joseph Andregg, who worked with Noss and attested to his discovery. To reporters, Andregg details once more the circumstances of his involvement with

Noss, about his having been at the peak when dynamite collapsed the shaft, about the gold bars and coins he observed Noss remove from the peak. He discloses he is here at the request of Mrs. Noss.

The project is halted for several hours when Scott sprains an arm in a fall into a 20-foot hole and is taken to a hospital. His arm in a sling, he returns to the site and work resumes at all points.

the fifth day ...

Only about half of the media representatives shows up today. Interest is beginning to lag.

There is a report the project is not going well at Bloody Hands. A Stanford Research Institute spokesman says ground radar has found an abnormality that might give rise to a tunnel, but "right now it's just a large void and it may be tough to excavate Geronimo Peak's hard rock to get to it."

Today there is a "hot" rumor that someone is planning to "salt" one of the crevices on Victoria Peak with a gold bar or two, and thus lay the groundwork for the sale of interests to the public. Much banter. Few put any credence in the rumor.

With members of family alongside her, Mrs. Noss (she is 81) climbs a steep, rocky path up Victoria Peak with the aid of two men. As the party reaches the top, Ova says, "If they had started digging here two days ago we would have already been in." Scott invites her to take a closer look at the Chimney entrance, thinking that it might refresh her memory of other leads to lower levels. She speaks of a rock doorway that Doc used to descend into Victoria Peak. "But it's been changed. It's been damaged quite a bit by someone." Before she left she pointed to other holes which she said were later used to try to gain access to the treasure trove.

A burst of excitement at the Bloody Hands dig — an archaeological find of importance! Removing rubble

208

blocking the entrance the crew comes upon man-made rock chips or "flakes" within a room-like formation. The chips may have been used by Indians as scrapers; one resembled an arrowhead. A Museum of New Mexico spokesman at the scene, Steve Koczan, seals off the cave and orders a stop to exploration until archaeologists can make a thorough scientific analysis. He tells reporters the artifacts prove the existence of cultural remains at the Bloody Hands, describes a clay layer bearing charcoal staining of a type that indicates prehistoric man could have built fires at the site.

Meanwhile at the Dome Room excavation workers use a backhoe to penetrate its roof in the hope of reaching a larger cavern.

the sixth day ...

The work at the Noss shaft atop Victoria Peak appears to be merely a perfunctory effort, much to the distress of Ova Noss.

Scott discloses his plan to open still another hold; the "burro" or "jackass" crevice in the northeast quadrant of Victoria. He says the Stanford people need to get their radar equipment closer to the Noss treasure rooms in order to obtain better readings. Deeper excavation at the burro hole would be helpful.

It is observed that individuals associated with the Bailey group do not make any move to reveal the location of the gold which they have contended would be within easy reach, once they were permitted on the range.

Comments critical of the Bailey group draw a reply from Bailey's law partner, Al Johnson:

"The official reason we did not produce gold in eleven hours or less is that the Army has filled in openings on the peak and screwed up the face of the mountain". His comments are interpreted as an attack on the military's "secret" explorations.

Scott announces he is now in a position to credit or discredit "definitely" the claims of several claimants as a result of the Stanford radar probes. He is reminded that he has only four days left. He replies he is confident he will have some basic observations by the tenth day.

Asked about rumors that a small cache of gold has been found near Victoria Peak, Scott replies: "The find was nothing more than a very small deposit of gold in the side of the tunnel. I can show you how to find gold in your backyard, but that doesn't mean there would be enough there to justify removing it."

The report that a salting of the search area might take place has surfaced again. We learn FBI agents have escorted two men from the Missile Range and told them not to return. The men are not identified but according to the FBI their plan was to plant a fake gold bar the size of a large candy bar in a place where it would be found by searchers.

The Army, through its public affairs officer, Major Kenneth Abel, discloses that the persons involved in the salting plan belonged to a certain claimant group. He did not name the group. The plan was thwarted by Army personnel acting on a tip from an undisclosed source.

Major Abel says "the Army did not turn anyone away. Their own group told them not to come back. I will not comment on how many people there were, but there were several and all in one party were asked to leave."

Scott says his injured arm is causing him severe pain, but will delay further medical attention until after the project.

We hear that Roscoe Parr and Violet Noss Yancy still refuse to take part in the project. Violet's lawyer, Jack Beach, is keeping in touch with the search effort from a hotel room in Las Cruces, N. M.

The number of press people has dwindled to a handful.

the seventh day . . .

210

It is Friday and the search is scheduled to end Monday.

Though the museum people have banned further work there, the operation at Bloody Hands is declared a failure. Two electronic probes yielded negative results.

Searchers are excavating a bat cave site about two-thirds up the north side of Victoria Peak, after a front-end loader scraped an opening into the mountain. In the cave, Scott says, they found "a circle with an arrow pointing down." He does not know the significance of the arrow, remarking: "It's probably pointing the way to the local McDonald's."

Also in the cave are large deposits of bat waste material, guano. The report is a signal for a puckish reporter to proclaim that Scott had found his treasure, at last. Guano, a fertilizer very rich in nitrates, is prized by farmers.

Today Scott makes a special plea to Ova Noss to assist in any way she can. He tells her that from this point on he is going to concentrate on the shaft entered by her former husband. He has tested the other locations without success and, looking back, he says he wishes he had devoted all the time to the Noss location. Scott considered it important to determine whether the other claims are valid, but now feels those claimants are sincere but "misguided."

Everyone here has an opinion on whether the treasure trove exists and whether it will be found. "Hell, no," says Major Abel, Army public relations, when asked about the treasure's existence. "This is the third time in sixteen years they've allowed a search at Victoria Peak and I hope the last time. Our business here is to test missiles, not hunt for gold."

the eighth day . . .

It is raining and cold. A strong, biting wind keeps virtually everyone in their motel rooms. Scott sends word that work for the day is cancelled. He is asking the Army to give him a day's extension. The request is granted.

Into the late afternoon hours yesterday the survey team, led by geophysicist Lambert Dolphin of the Stanford Research Institute, roved the Victoria Peak area conducting more scientific tests.

Elsewhere near the peak another team is using metal detectors, following leads given them by a man named Tony Jolly, who says he was with Noss when he buried 110 bars of gold the night before Noss was shot.

Scott says, "In my opinion there is no question that gold-like bars came out of this mountain. There are too many affidavits and too much research to contend otherwise."

the ninth day ...

Sunday. Few reporters on hand. Little activity at the peak. Some snow has fallen but the bad weather is tapering off. Exploration period will end at sundown Tuesday.

Scott admits he is behind schedule but says "the purpose of this mission will be accomplished by Monday," apparently falling back on his original plan — to find voids, not search for gold. Some feel it is a convenient alibi in the event he finds no gold.

The men who went down the Noss shaft say it goes at least a hundred feet before the plug of fill dirt is reached, blocking the connection with the main passage to the treasure rooms.

It is the same one which Ova Noss has been insisting connects with the cave in which Noss found the gold.

Dolphin calls the shaft the "best bet" to reach the rooms inside the mountain. "If we can get the plug out in time, then we might be in the original Noss room." His team is using ground radar to probe the area around the shaft. Readings confirm the earlier estimate that the

212

fill is about 30 feet deep.

Ova agrees with Dolphin. "I've always said that if they want to get to the treasure they should use the same route Doc used."

In response to Scott's request for cooperation Ova decides she will produce charts drawn by Doc Noss himself. The charts are in her trailer home in Clovis, so Scott arranges for a private plane to take her there and return in time for the start of work tomorrow morning. It is rumored Scott has agreed to pay her a substantial sum for the charts, but Scott angrily denies it.

Mrs. Noss came today with a large family album, showed workers and military police early photographs of the peak and her family in the days when they were scooping debris from the shaft.

Scott discloses he is able to discount the existence of seven of the nine major caves — claims which he has been pursuing all week. Now he can prove "conclusively" that the seven are "actually not based on fact." He says he is doubtful they will be able to penetrate the clogged portion of the Noss shaft, estimating that it would take at least fifty man-hours, possibly more.

The Army makes no secret of the fact that they are tired of the whole business, exhibiting an air of humorless resignation as they go about the daily chore of ferrying the visitors to and from the search area.

the tenth day ...

Renewed effort to remove the 30-foot plug of rocks and dirt in the vertical shaft. The work continues by hand. Debris is taken out in buckets. Workers not optimistic the task can be accomplished in the remaining days.

Scott says he may ask for a further extension.

Expeditions Unlimited surveyors are pleased with the sketches loaned them by Ova Noss. The radar scans so far confirm their correctness. Sam Scott, brother of Norman Scott, points out, "If the Noss story holds after excavation and more tests then I think it's pretty conclusive that something's down there — and still is."

Dolphin of the Museum says the Noss sketches were made by persons untrained in geology but "are consistent with the geology of the area."

the eleventh day . . .

Only a day more. Crews are working frantically at the Noss shaft, using a jackhammer to shatter rock that cannot be removed by hand. Scott says they are trying to excavate a cubic foot of debris each hour but doubts that the pace can be maintained. At least twenty feet of rubble remain.

Scott says, "We should have attacked the Noss shaft when we first came. It was a goof, perhaps, but an honest one."

The total concentration on the Noss claim cancels other locations — Soldier's Hole, Bloody Hands, Dome, Bat Cave, Donkey's Hole. They were among the more vigorously pursued, now abandoned for one reason or another.

Crewmen are able to lower electronic equipment to a level more than a hundred feet deep in the Noss shaft. *Soundings appear to confirm the existence of a large cavern inside the peak at a much deeper level.*

Scott receives another extension of time from the base command office. Now he has until 5 p.m. Friday. Four more days.

A limited expedition planned in the so-called Vaughn area south of Victoria Peak is cancelled because the claimants cannot recall the exact location where some gold bars were allegedly buried.

Excavation crews continue to work with hand tools in the Noss shaft while other expedition members are busy closing excavations at other locations.

214

Scott shows us a map which he says depicts the "exact location and dimensions" of the mountain for the first time in its history. The map is based on a series of ground radar tests conducted by Stanford Research in the past ten days.

He says the Noss legend might have been solved in 1963 if the Gaddis Mining company in its exploration on Victoria Peak had dug 30 feet to the right of its original excavation.

We learn Ova's daughter, Letha Guthrie, has led a small group into a canyon near the peak in search of a cache of twenty-six gold bars buried by Doc Noss within walking distance of a dirt road that skirts Victoria Peak. She says, "He just moved some rocks and threw them in. He was probably close to the road."

Using metal detectors two men scan a number of rocky arroyo beds suggested by Mrs. Guthrie but the search is abandoned after a few hours.

the twelfth day ...

The announcement at this morning's press conference is no surprise. Scott says they are giving up, the search is over. He gives a reason: With the limited time available, removing the rubble would take a major excavation. Besides, the Army would not allow another extension "unless the Noss family has tangible proof of the Noss claim or gold or both."

the thirteenth day ...

Scott appears at the site an hour and a half later than usual this morning. He tells reporters, "There will be no further activities of Expeditions Unlimited beyond today on the search site."

The workers will start cleaning up and demobilizing. "Operation Goldfinder" has ended.

The last press conference

Visibly weary, face drawn from pain in the injured arm, Scott visits with a small group of reporters. He has a few final remarks which he says are tentative, until Expeditions Unlimited and the Stanford Institute can prepare a formal report on the project, possibly within thirty days.

He does not consider the mission a failure. On the contrary, "Our objectives were realized — with one possible exception."

The exception is the Noss claim. He cannot say with scientific certainty there is gold there. Nor can he say there is not. But they were able to determine there was "no treasure in various locations where most of the claimants told us a gold cache is hidden."

He says they did document the existence of a large cavern near the Noss shaft, adding:

"That's still a mystery. The real dilemma in the whole picture. And it won't be solved until someone is willing to spend a fortune excavating the blocked shaft and crevices."

His next disclosure is startling in the extreme to a few present not acquainted with Fiege's discovery of gold bars.

"We believe Captain Fiege's story is factual. We think he did enter a cave in Victoria Peak."

There is a good feeling about the way Scott managed the project, prudent and careful to prevent whatever would give the search a circus atmosphere.

He told them, "I wish I could come before you and

say the answers are positively yes or positively no. But it's impossible to state that because it is beyond the scope of our mission. Unfortunately and regrettably, the claimants and their sources were misinformed. We found no gold in the exact spots identified by these claimants."

Scott said he himself believes Ova Noss' claim that Doc Noss found an entrance into Victoria Peak that led to a large cavern. "Is there gold in that cavern? We have no idea whatsoever."

He has no plans to attempt further exploration. It would require a major mining expedition and an investment of thousands of dollars to confirm whether Victoria Peak holds any gold bullion. This effort, he said, cost $87,000.

"It is very, very difficult to put legends to rest. Everybody wants to find gold, including yours truly. It was a short experience that we enjoyed. And the dust baths we got were very refreshing."

He then read from a preliminary report prepared by Lambert Dolphin of Stanford Research, quoting: "The mystery of where the gold originally came from, if in fact it ever did, still remains as to this day."

Jim Delonas, a grandson of Mrs. Noss, said the Noss family believes the Scott expedition was beneficial in "putting to rest the many claims by intermeddlers."

Maj. Ken Abel, WSMR public affairs officer, issued a brief statement:

"WSMR is now closed to further search. This exploration in conjunction with two previous efforts over the past 16 years indicates no treasure, gold or otherwise, exists in the area of Hembrillo Basin or Victoria Peak."

Scott discloses he would not consider returning for a second try without strong financing and a much longer work period, estimating it would cost a half million dollars and take two months to complete the excavation of the Noss shaft.

The general attitude of the reporters was reflected by John Crewdson's article in The New York Times a few days later:

> *"Scott's failure will probably serve only to enhance the Noss legend, since Dolphin's ground-penetrating radar device indicated the presence of a cavern far down inside the limestone mountain, just about where Doc Noss said it was."*

The still unsolved aspect of the exploration preyed on Lambert Dolphin's mind in the following months. In July he filed with the Missile Range commandant a request that the Stanford Research Institute be allowed to conduct another search at Victoria Peak, financed through exclusive sale of film footage to a television network, to "find the stacks of gold bullion, coins and artifacts that legend says is buried in the mountain," requiring 90 days and using heavy excavation equipment to reach "a huge cavern located 450 feet underneath Victoria Peak."

The Army said it was not interested in still another search and no permit would be granted.

The Stanford officials hastened to explain they had not made a formal request but more to sound out the Army's attitude toward another try at the peak. The significance of Stanford's continued interest, however, pointed to the weakness of the Army's adamantine insistence that no treasure exists, or ever did exist, at Victoria Peak. Stanford's faith apparently was such as to justify a further attempt to reach the treasure rooms, something that still remains the crux of the Noss riddle.

Not quiet for long

The behavior of Doc Noss and Captain Fiege is a study in the vagaries of human judgment. They might have achieved great wealth had they publicly disclosed the nature of their discovery to the appropriate authorities. But their course of action, designed to protect the treasure, actually cast a legal shadow over it.

Fiege's behavior is almost inexplicable. First, he allowed a considerable treasure in gold to remain in the cave for a considerable period, thus reflecting a stoutness of spirit of which few men are capable. He was able to let the months and years flow by with the knowledge that a vast fortune was within easy reach behind a thin wall of debris.

Other questions surge into the mind.

How simple to escort a Treasury or Secret Service operative to the scene, with an attorney at his side, proclaim his title to it as an original finder and, resting, await the law of treasure trove to test his claim.

Or he might have elected, if he were less conscientious, to spirit the treasure away in the small of the night, and arrange to dispose of it in the black market or other sources so accessible in that shady field of back-alley commerce.

Further, one may speculate on his failure to mark the location of the cave by discreet placement of a rod or piece of timber. If not that precaution, then a well-outlined map of the immediate area — a device so much a part of lost-gold literature from time immemorial.

For an answer to some of these riddles, I set about seeking an opportunity to contact Fiege. My initial efforts to obtain his current address through official Air Force sources were futile; such information, I was told, is confidential, available only with the consent of the addressee.

My next step was to follow the Air Force's instructions: Prepare a letter to Captain Fiege, place it in an envelope along with a check for $2.80 payable to the Air Force and send it to a specific Air Force office, which in turn would transmit our letter to Fiege. If the addressee wishes, he will respond.

In my case Fiege apparently did not wish to respond; I heard nothing. So, distressing as it may be to many, the vexatious questions surrounding Fiege's discovery of the treasure and his subsequent behavior remain unanswered, awaiting some distant day of clarification.

Or perhaps the Fiege case does not need explanation.

His discovery and his creation of a corporation in association with Colonel Gasiewicz and others are not the ingredients of some wives' tale shrouded in the mists of ancient history. They are entries sworn to and on the record. They contribute meaningfully to the sequence of events at Victoria Peak — despite the Army's public posture of indifference to the entire Noss experience and its stubborn edict: "There is not now and there never was a treasure trove at Victoria Peak."

I employed the same procedure, with the Air Force acting as the transmitting agent, in an effort to reach Colonel Gasiewicz, at this writing retired and living in Florida. It succeeded. On the day of our telephone conversation in the fall of '82, Mrs. Gasiewicz revealed the colonel was "quite ill." However, she was well acquainted with the Fiege situation, having gone through it, she said, "step by step with the colonel". She told us she would be happy to discuss any aspect of it. And proceeded to do so at some length, in a spirited, articulate manner. She quickly made it clear that while both she and the colonel were skeptical in the early phase of their acquaintance with Fiege, "we never thought it wise to turn our back on his story."

She related how Fiege excitedly poured out his story to Colonel Gasiewicz at the time of the discovery and that there was much discussion among them thereafter. The colonel convinced Fiege that the matter should be handled properly — through channels in Washington. The colonel then arranged for the two of them, with Berlett and others, to meet there with officials of the Treasury department.

Mrs. Gasiewicz continued:

"Well, at the meeting in Washington the Treasury people took the attitude they would go through this one more time. They knew all about the Noss case and wheeled out a cart loaded with files and documents going back to the early years. It was suggested Fiege and Berlett take lie-detector tests. They did and the tests showed they were telling the truth about finding stacks of gold bars at Victoria Peak.

"Now of course when this happened we're a good deal more interested and Colonel Gasiewicz who is an expert at that sort of thing told them they should form a corporation. There were seven of them in all, and the colonel wrote up the incorporation papers, I typed them and they were filed. The group agreed none of them would enter into any sort of arrangement with any outsider relating to the treasure while the corporation was in existence. You see, the incorporation was to protect their title to the gold in the event it was removed by someone else.

"That's why the colonel didn't feel it was necessary for him to be present at the search project by Norman Scott in 1977. We felt that whatever they found would have to undergo a court test and we would be able then to make our own case. It's one of those situations where you build up a lot of files and clippings, but you don't throw them away. You just hang in there, and when the subject comes up, as it does every five or ten years, why you just break out the files and enjoy the whole thing over again."

My last contact with Norman Scott of Expeditions Unlimited was at Victoria Peak during the 1977 exploration. Knowing him as a man of strong opinion and incisive attitude I felt it was time to seek out his final conclusions on the Noss case after the passing of these five years.

The renewal by telephone was warm and friendly. He had formulated a number of interesting opinions; one disclosure, if true, provided an answer to Fiege's silence. Scott said Fiege died within a year after the 1977 project. (But it would be only a few months later that another source would advise us that Fiege was alive and well.)

As to Doc Noss:

"Noss did find a treasure but not as large as it has been made out to be . . ."

Also:

"Fiege found gold bars at Victoria Peak. He was telling the truth. However, I think he removed a few bars from the cave, enough to tide him over until the whole matter could be processed quietly through the military."

Then he said:

"I have a hypothetical solution to the mystery of where most of the gold came from. I'm speaking of the gold that is in addition to the Noss treasure. But make it clear my opinion is just a hypothesis. I have no proof of it or any documentation to back it up."

"Here is it: Patton's army in their march through Germany came upon a tremendous amount of gold and shipped it back to this country. Twenty-nine members of Patton's staff elected to settle at the White Sands Missile Range after the war, when they could have chosen any one of a number of better billets. They hid the German gold in and around Victoria Peak. Why? Because Victoria Peak already had a convenient treasure trove legend and if anyone discovered the German gold in the military's possession, all the military had to do was say it was part of the Noss treasure. Simple as that. But as I say, this is just a personal opinion. I will not say why I believe it has considerable basis in reality. I should add that the Army, on the highest possible level, was well aware that a treasure of gold existed at White Sands. I mean levels higher than the White Sands command office."

The Noss case's bottom-line query is today what it was twenty-three years ago when I first became entwined in its glittering toils.

Did Doc Noss really come upon a treasure in Victoria Peak?

I am convinced he did.

There is much too much flesh on the bones of this legend to classify it with the old or ancient tales of lost treasures that crowd library shelves.

Anyone seeking a rationale may view the Noss mystery in this light:

..... the scores of individuals who professed their faith in Doc Noss and put it in writing.

..... The witnesses and fellow workers who saw the gold in Doc's hands and were certain it was the real stuff.

..... the officials of the Gaddis Mining company of Denver who spent almost a quarter of a million dollars at Victoria Peak in support of their belief in the existence of the treasure.

..... the Salt Lake City group who gave $25,000 for a percentage of Ova Noss' interest, after seeing what they identified as gold bars taken from the Noss caverns.

..... the enigmatic figure of Charley Ryan whose involvement led to homicide.

..... Air Force pilot Fiege's exciting find that drew a seasoned attorney like Colonel Gasiewicz into formal partnership, inspired by supportive lie-detector tests.

..... F. Lee Bailey, his 50 unidentified clients, his secret overtures played out heavy-handedly against the background of White House influence.

..... Expeditions Unlimited and the 1977 probe, which left unanswered the key question: What still remains in the treasure caverns, whose location was pinpointed scientifically by Stanford Research Institute.

..... Norman Scott's and the New Mexico Museum's report that the cave deep in Victoria Peak is exactly where Noss and his family have always insisted it is.

The above listing is merely a leap from one peak to another, a recitation of some of the more compelling elements in the case. Not in the list, however, is a most persuasive aspect — the lifelong dedication of Ova Noss herself. From 1937 to her death in the spring of 1980 she resorted to every strategy available to a person of her means. She was not cunning, being a plain, direct woman. Time and again she found herself in the bureaucratic strangle of a society that does not always provide equal opportunity. The Noss story would have yielded up its secrets had the Army assisted Ova in excavating the shaft — using the money it later spent in secret and futile efforts to reach the gold.

What ultimate fate, then, is in store for the controversy engendered by the three-quarter blood Cheyenne from Oklahoma?

To treasure seekers and adventurers the lure of gold and ancient artifacts is much too tantalizing to resist.

224

Their devotion to such a cause is greatly intensified, however, when the drama has reality and a piercing logic coupled with a contemporary cast of characters. The Noss discovery offers all these ingredients along with a conviction among its numerous believers that the bulk of the gold is still within the peak. Between the treasure and the deprived claimants stands the military, a petulant and despotic behemoth flexing its bureaucratic sinews; all the more irritating in its refusal to allow an adequate exploration while secretly conducting its own search activities at the peak.

True it is that the military command at White Sands is enjoying a respite from the anguished outcries of the faithful. But the mystery will fret and continue to fester upon its conscience, making less tenable the thin disguise of interference with missile testing. The mystery at Victoria Peak is their special agony. It is my surmise that claimants will continue to cram-throat authorities in Washington until one day the military will release its maniacally possessive hold on Victoria Peak.

Meanwhile regional historians have given the Noss discovery an honor which they strongly feel it deserves — a place among the great legends of the Southwest. If, as some skeptics say, it is a modern folk tale, it has not behaved like one. For one thing appears certain — it will not remain quiet for long. Nor has it in the several decades since its origin, rising each time with new vigor and plausibility — enchanting its followers and forcing a deeper reflection on the evidences of its reality.

When it returns again, as it surely will, perhaps there will take place another manifestation, like the one so plaintively voiced by the Washington Post during the 1977 effort to free the spirit of ol' Doc Noss:

VICTORIA PEAK, N.M., June 20 - If a ghostly cackle of laughter rings across this desolate limestone outcrop these days, it's only Doc Noss chuckling over yet another try at unearthing his legendary billion-dollar treasure trove.

One day in early spring, several months before her death, Ova telephoned to, as she put it, "visit with my old lawyer friend." The treasure was still uppermost in her mind but her words revealed a new and deeper anguish; what really did happen to all that gold? Quickly, she provided her own answer. "Maybe you can't prove it and maybe I can't prove it but let me tell you this, maybe Army people got it. If they didn't, then most of it is still down in Victoria Peak."

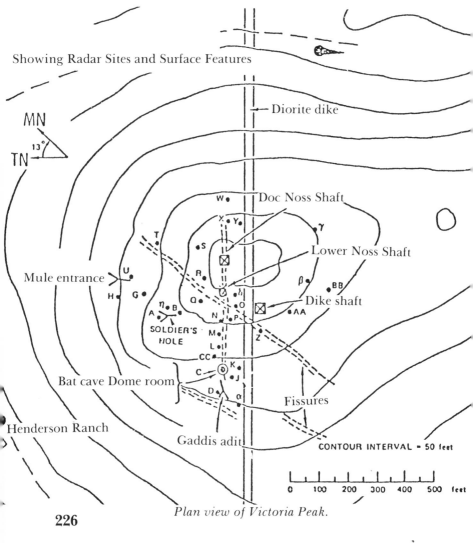

Plan view of Victoria Peak.

Whose Gold is it?

If, as fate may have decreed, Doc Noss left behind a great treasure, he also created a maze of legal questions centered on the question of ownership of the gold. Each claimant's position has some basis in logic stemming from an act on the individual's part, or on a concession granted by Noss or his family. Together, the claims are an interlacery of opposing contentions certain ultimately to draw the parties into prolonged litigation.

The legal cases on ownership of treasure trove are not in themselves all that complicated. In truth, there is much in the law from which specific ground rules can be drawn.

The examples are many, all pointing to an unusual unity of opinion. A leading case on the subject involved two Maine workmen who uncovered a large crock of old coins while digging on the householder's property. They refused to surrender the coins, contending the cache was theirs under the law. The householder brought suit.

The court supported the position of the workmen in a ruling that reflects the settled law on treasure trove — the finder of treasure trove acquires a title that is good against all the world *except the true owner.*

In the instant case the householder urged the theory that the land and the dirt were his, that he was entitled to whatever was contained or buried therein. Not so, said the court: "The place where the treasure is found is immaterial. The owner of the soil in which the treasure trove is found acquires no title thereto by virtue of his ownership of land."

That sentence was taken verbatim by the court from the old English common law case of Armory V. Delamarie, which for several centuries has set the tone and logic of treasure trove controversies. The individual who buried the gold is the only one with a title superior to that of the finder. (Treasure trove, in the accepted view, is any gold or silver in coin, plate or bullion found concealed in the earth or in a house or other private place, but not lying openly on the ground, the owner of the discovered treasure being unknown.)

Many years ago, not far from the writer's home, under circumstances similar to those of the above discovery, workmen found valuable, uncirculated gold coins more than a hundred years old in an old crock concealed in dirt that had been trucked to the property in preparation for construction of a garage. The workmen, not knowing their rights, surrendered the valuable coins to the householder, who sincerely believed the coins were properly his.

In some cases courts have ruled that "finders" did not become true finders because they failed to *reduce their find to possession.* Anyone researching this aspect of the law inevitably is led to a controversy that occurred in Arkansas in 1861. A boat with a cargo of lead bars sank in the Mississippi river and was abandoned by its owners. Several years later it was discovered by two men, who placed a buoy over the spot with the intent to remove the lead in a few weeks, at the time having a work commitment in another area. While the two workers were thus engaged elsewhere, another party found the sunken boat and began removing the lead. Rejecting the claims of the first finders, the court wrote a lengthy discourse on what constitutes a true finder, saying in part, "The occupation or possession of property lost, abandoned or without an owner, must depend upon an actual taking of the property and with the intent to reduce it to possession .... The first 'finders' never attained to the possession of the sunken boat, therefore had no title to it by occupancy . . . . They had the intention of possessing it as owners, but did not acquire its corporeal possession . . . . Marking trees that extended across the wreck, affixing temporary buoys to it, were not acts of possession; they only indicated their desire or intention to appropriate the property. But placing their boat over the wreck, with the means to raise its valuables (would be) such acts of possession the law would notice and protect."

The principle of these decisions, meaningful in the Noss situation, enables the first finder to prevail over subsequent finders. After Doc Noss' death and while Mrs. Noss was seeking possession, military personnel revealed there had been a discovery of gold bars at the Missile Range. In a legal confrontation, the issue would center on whether the first discovery by Noss is sufficient to establish ownership as against any subsequent finder.

Virtually without exception the cases support Noss' position as owner of the gold bars which he removed from the caverns and hid in various places in and near the peak. In the legal phrase, he "reduced the property to possession." He made them his own with a distinct proprietary act — and they are his in the absence of a claim by the true owner, i.e., the party who put them there in the first instance.

Immediately there is a sequential — and perhaps more tantalizing — question: What is the legal status of the treasures sealed off and unreachable as a result of the dynamite blast?

Do they belong to Noss, thus ruling out entitlement by a subsequent finder?

Or may it be said he abandoned the cavern treasures after the collapse, when he failed to make timely application for permits to continue exploration?

Once again the cases support his position. He had in-hand possession when he went into the caverns and removed some of the bars. Such possession would constitute him a finder of all the bullion in the caves. Furthermore, like the salvage ship positioned over the sunken river vessel, Noss worked over and in the most direct channel by which the bullion could be reached; such actions are legally sufficient to justify his claim of ownership. On the basis of these circumstances, the gold bars found and retained by military personnel are the rightful property of the heirs and assigns of "Doc" Noss.

Now, as to Ova Noss, first as sole enterpriser and, secondly, as Doc Noss' former wife. Obviously, in these considerations note must be taken of a formidable figure waiting in the wings, Violet Noss Yancy, Doc Noss' wife at the time of his death.

Ova was with Noss at the time of the discovery and as his wife was entitled to a part of it, as much as 50%, according to statutes in some jurisdictions. Also, she had the right to a half of the bars hidden by her husband. If someone else chanced upon these hidden caches their right to them would be subject or inferior to Ova's.

It therefore follows that if Fiege or other military

230

personnel did come upon these caches and remove them they did so in violation of Ova's rights.

After Doc's death, Ova returned to the peak with her family to attempt to excavate the shaft. Over a period of years she was given the proper permits and, had she reached the treasure rooms, would have had good basis to claim title to at least half, if not all, of their contents.

These actions on Ova's part would seem to rule out the legitimacy of the claim by Doc's widow, Violet, that 76% of all that Doc found belongs to her.

It appears at this precise moment that Violet's claim would not be valid. Her marriage to Doc came at a point in time when he no longer was at the peak, having been replaced by Ova and her family. However, in the absence of a premarital property agreement, Violet is entitled to her one-half statutory allowance to whatever Doc owned at the time of his death.

The airman, Capt. Leonard V. Fiege, remains the most enigmatic of all the figures in the Victoria Peak scenario. His own sworn affidavit and the results of the subsequent lie-detector test, leave little doubt that he did find gold bars in a cavern in Victoria Peak. He said he did not remove any of the bars, that he collapsed the entrance to prevent their discovery by anyone else, and later returned to the site with other personnel in an exploration approved and supervised by the military command. The search did not succeed in locating the entrance to the cave and Fiege, we must assume, profited not a cent from his multimillion-dollar discovery.

On a legal basis, his actions did not constitute reducing his find to possession; in fact, he abandoned the treasure almost as quickly as he had chanced upon it and would therefore be precluded from a successful claim. Further, if what he found was a cache hidden by Doc Noss his title would be inferior to that held by Doc and Ova.

***

A legal footnote

The finder .... the possessor .... the claimant ....
UNDER THE LAW
OF TREASURE TROVE

I. TREASURE TROVE BELONGS TO THE FINDER.

The general American rule, which is derived from the English common law, is that the finder of treasure trove acquires the title and possessory rights against all except the true owner. These rights are even superior to those of the owner of the premises upon which the treasure trove is found. For instance, in *Weeks vs. Hackett,* 71 Atl. 858, 104 Me. 264 (1908), two workmen uncovered old buried coins on the defendant's property. The court held that the coins belonged to the workmen, stating at page 860:

"... the general rule is established by a substantially uniform line of decisions in the American states, ... that, in the absence of legislation upon the subject, the title to such property belongs to the finder as against all the world except the true owner, and that ordinarily the place where it is found is immaterial. ... The owner of the soil in which treasure trove is found acquires no title thereto by virtue of his ownership of land."

Furthermore, in *Niederlehner vs. Weatherly,* 69 NE 2d 787, 78 Ohio App. 264, a vagrant claimed that he found money in a house, owned by one who predicated her claim upon such ownership, while a third claimant argued that it was originally his money and that he hid it there. In sustaining the latter's contention, the court rejected the landowner's claim at page 791:

"Neither can she prevail if the funds be treasure trove, for the reason that since the time of Armory vs. Delamarie, 1 Strange 505, 93 English Reports (22 King's Bench) 664, it has been the law, that the owner of the premises whereon treasure is buried acquires no title or right thereto by virtue thereof, as against the finder or the true owner."

Accord: *Danielson vs. Roberts,* 44 Ore 108, 74 Pac 913; *Zech vs. Accola,* 253 Wisc 80, 33 NW 2d 232, *Zorens vs. Bowan,* 223 Iowa 1141, 274 NW 877. Therefore, under these authorities, the finder of treasure trove is entitled to ownership and possession against the world at large, except for the true owner of the treasure. However, since there are no New Mexico statutes or cases in this area, and since, according to *In Re: Chavez,* 149 Fed. 73, the source of New Mexico case law is Spanish and Mexican civil law, there may be a shred of doubt about whether this general rule, with English common law roots, is the New Mexico law.

II. TREASURE TROVE DEFINED.

The "treasure trove" to which the above rule applies is defined in *Weeks vs. Hackett,* supra, at page 859:

"'Treasure trove' is a name given by the early common law to any gold or silver in coin, plate, or bullion found concealed in the earth, or in a house or other private place, but not lying on the ground; the owner of the discovered treasure being unknown."

This definition is universal. See *Zech vs. Accola,* supra; *Groover vs. Tippins,* 51 Ga. App. 447, 179 SE 634; *Vickery vs. Hardin,* 77 Ind. App. 558, 133 NE 922; 36A C.J.S., Finding Lost Goods, Section 1, Page 418. Therefore, there appears to be little doubt that the alleged treasure in this case constitutes treasure trove, to which the above general rule probably applies.

III. FINDER DEFINED.

The real crux of this case is whether or not Noss became a "finder". The leading American case on this problem is *Eads vs. Brazelton,* 22 Ark. 449, 79 Am. Dec. 88 (1861). In this case, a boat with a cargo of shot and lead bars sank in the Mississippi River and was abandoned by its owners. Several years later, the plaintiff found it and placed a buoy over it with the intent to recover the lead, but he was delayed in further pursuing the recovery because of work commitments elsewhere. Nine months later, the defendant found the sunken hull and placed his boat over it and started removing the lead. The plantiff claimed that he was entitled to the cargo as the original finder. However, the court held that the defendant rather than the plaintiff was a finder. The court, after examining the leading English cases and commentaries, presented a lucid discourse on the elements of finding at pages 509, 511 and 512:

"The occupation or possession of property lost, abandoned, or without an owner, must depend upon an actual taking of the property and with the intent to reduce it to possession. The intent may not be that this possession shall be in absolute or perpetual appropriation of the property to the use of the finder, it may be subject to the claim of the real owner, the possession may be taken for his exclusive good, or it may be taken as a means of subsistence or accumulation, according to the course of business of the parties to this suit. But in any case, title by occupancy must rest upon intentional actual possession of the thing occupied.

* * * * *

". . . and the rule as stated by him is to this effect; *that to acquire possession of a thing there must be a desire to possess it, joined to a prehension of the thine.* (Citations)

* * * * *

". . . we hold that Brazelton never attained to the possession of the wreck of the America, that he therefore had no title to it by occupancy, and no right upon which judicial protection could operate, none which the court below should have recognized. He had considered the wreck as his as its finder, but had not actually appropriated it to himself; his intention to possess was useless without detention of the property; he had not found the lead in the required sense of discovering it, and taking it up; he was not a finder, in that he had not moved the wrecked property or secured it; he had the intention of possessing it as owner, but did not acquire its corporeal possession; to his desire to possess there was not joined a prehension of the thing.

"Brazelton's act of possession need not have been manual, he was not obliged to take the wreck or the lead between his hands, *he might take such possession of them as their nature and situation permitted;* but that his circumstances should give a legal character to his acts, making that to be possession which the law declares not to be possession, assumes more than a court can sanction. Marking trees that extended across the wreck, affixing temporary buoy's to it, were not acts of possession; they only indicated Brazelton's desire or intention to appropriate the property. *Placing his boat over the wreck, with the means to raise its valuables, and with persistent efforts directed to raising the lead, would have been keeping the only effectual guard over it,* would have been the only warning that intruders, that is, other longing occupants, would be obliged to regard, *would have been such acts of possession as the law would notice and protect."* (Emphasis added)

Accord: *Lawrence vs. Buck,* 62 Me. 275; 36A C.J.S., Finding Lost Goods, Section 2. Thus, under the ruling of this leading American case, a finder must have both the intent to possess and the best means of possession possible under the particular circumstances. It is evident from the facts of these two cases that in-hand possession is not the absolute prerequisite if that is not possible at the time. One can have possession by exercising such a degree of exclusive control as to preclude others from having access to the treasure. There seems to be little question in our case that Noss had the required intent. According to the facts as I understand them, at one time Dr. Noss had in-hand possession when he went into the cave and removed some bars. It would seem that such possession would be sufficient possession of all of the bullion in that cave to constitute him a finder. Furthermore, like the salvage ship positioned over the sunken river vessel, Dr. Noss worked over and in the most direct channel by which the bullion could be reached; this in itself would constitute possession and would make him a finder under the terms of the *Brazelton* case. If a finder's rights of ownership and possession are inheritable, then they inured to Mrs. Noss, and she perhaps enjoys such rights by inheritance or devise. On the other hand, if a finder's status and rights do not pass by inheritance, it would

234

seem, nevertheless, that Mrs. Noss is a finder in her own right. Following her husband's death, Mrs. Noss, with the requisite intent to possess and own, located and pursued the excavation over the blocked shaft, which was the most direct route to the treasure trove; this is the best possible possession and control under the circumstances, and is very analogous to the *Brazelton* case. That she did not ultimately reduce the bullion once again to physical possession would seem to be of no consequence, since she was forcibly prevented from doing so by the federal government.

IV. THE FIRST FINDER PREVAILS OVER SUBSEQUENT FINDERS.

Whether the servicemen are finders of the remainder of the bullion within the standards of the *Brazelton* case may be open to some question; not enough of the facts are known to draw a conclusion on this. Nevertheless, even if they are finders, as subsequent finders they are inferior to Mrs. Noss. This was the holding of *Deaderick vs. Oulds,* 86 Tenn. 14, 5 SW 487, where the defendant found a strange, lost log while searching for his own logs which had strayed while floating downsteam to a mill. He included this log in his new log boom which he sent on downstream. However, when this new boom broke and the logs scattered, the lost log landed on the plaintiff's property and he claimed it as a finder. The court held that the defendant was entitled to that log with these words at page 488:

> "The prior finding and possession of the defendant is sufficient, not only to defeat the contention of the plaintiff, but was a sufficient title to have supported an action of replevin to recover the possession from any but the true owner."

The prior finder also prevailed in *Lawrence vs. Buck,* supra, and *Agnew vs. Baker,* 204 Ill. App. 56 (1917); see 36A C.J.S., Finding Lost Goods, Section 5(e), page 424. Therefore, Mrs. Noss, as a prior finder, is entitled to the possession and ownership of the bullion as against the servicemen, who are subsequent finders at best.

V. THE ENGLISH STATUTE MAKING THE STATE OWNER OF TREASURE TROVE IS INAPPLICABLE.

According to the court in *Danielson vs. Roberts,* supra, the statute of 4 Edward 1 vested the treasure trove title in the Crown subject to the claims of the true owner. The court in that case stated at page 914:

> "It (treasure trove) originally belonged to the finder if the owner was not discovered; but Blackstone says it was afterward adjudged expedient for the purposes of the state, and particularly for the coinage, that it should go to the King; and so the rule was promulgated that property found . . . hidden in the earth belonged to the King. 1 Blackstone Commentaries No. 295."

Nevertheless, that case sustained the finder's trover action. Furthermore, no American decision has denied a finder's claim to treasure trove on the theory that title to such was vested in the state; indeed, all of the cases cited above, although professing to apply the English common law, awarded the ownership and possession of treasure trove to the finder. Thus, it appears that American courts are applying the English common law as it existed prior to the statute.

Furthermore, it is arguable that that statute is of no consequence under the locale and facts of this case. Perhaps the civil law basis of New Mexico's case law precludes the application of the English statute, although such an argument might jeopardize the application of the treasure trove doctrine itself. Furthermore, since New Mexico has granted and would again grant permission to Mrs. Noss to recover the treasure trove, it appears that the state has delegated any ownership rights it may have to Mrs. Noss. Hence, she has a cognizable ownership claim.

VI. WHETHER THE LAW OF LOST PROPERTY AND TREASURE TROVE ARE MERGED IS OF NO CONSEQUENCE.

The court in *Danielson vs. Roberts*, supra, in the course of awarding treasure trove to the finder as opposed to the landowner, stated at page 914:

> "In this country the law relating to treasure trove has generally been merged into the law of the finder of lost property . . . ."

However, there is not complete agreement that such is the case, for in *Zech vs. Acolla,* supra, where the defendant sought to defeat the plaintiff's claim to treasure trove on the ground that the latter failed to give the notice required by the "lost property statute", the court awarded the treasure trove to the finder with the statement that the statute did not apply. Nevertheless, we need not concern ourselves with this problem, for as noted in *Zech vs. Acolla,* supra, in either event possession of such property belongs to the finder against all except the true owner. See statements to the same effect in *Hill vs. Schrunk,* 292 Pac 2d 141 (Ore. 1956); *Jackson vs. Steinberg,* 186 Ore. 129, 200 Pac 2d 376 (1948); *Schley vs. Couch,* 284 SW 2d 333 (Texas, 1955).

VII. TEXAS' REJECTION OF TREASURE TROVE MAY NOT BE APPLICABLE TO OUR CASE.

Neighboring Texas has rejected the treasure trove theory according to the language of *Schley vs. Couch,* supra. The plaintiff in that case, finding money in a glass jar while doing construction work on the defendant's premises, claimed it as a finder of treasure trove. The court stated at page 335 that they had decided to reject the treasure trove doctrine and that the cases should be governed by the rules of law applicable to lost and mislaid property. The court expressly recognized that treasure trove was the American majority rule and that its roots were firmly anchored in the English common law, but they gave no real reason for not recognizing the doctrine, save only that "we can see no good reason at the present time and under present conditions in our nation, to adopt such a doctrine." The concurring justice pointedly objected to this portion of the decision, because he saw no circumstances in Texas justifying the rejection of the

236

American majority rule with English common law roots. Certainly if the treasure trove doctrine is applicable in Georgia, which was the home of Blackbeard and Captain Kidd, *Groover vs. Tippins,* supra, it would seem to be applicable in New Mexico which is the site of many buried treasures of the conquistadores. However, if the source of New Mexico case law is the civil law of Spain and Mexico, then there is a logical basis for denying the application of a rule of law which has English common law roots. Nevertheless, there are many bases for arguing that the *Schley* case is not precedent for New Mexico in this situation. For instance, in that case the dispute was between the finder and the landowner, while our case involves two finders. Furthermore, that case eventually awarded the property to the owner of the premises on the theory that it was mislaid property, which is a category presently existing under the majority American rule. Also, that case involved paper currency rather than gold, coins or bullion, and as noted in 36A C.J.S., Finding Lost Goods, Section 1, there is still some dispute whether paper currency is treasure trove. In addition, that case expresses a minority view which is in direct contradiction to the general American doctrines. Finally, the bullion in our case was not found on privately owned land, as was the money in that case.

VIII. THE BULLION IS PROBABLY NOT MISLAID PROPERTY.

There is a tendency among the courts to rule that buried money is neither lost property nor treasure trove but is mislaid property. For instance, in *Schley vs. Couch,* supra, where the buried currency was in a glass jar and was only four years old, the court defined lost property as:

"'That which the owner has involuntarily parted with through neglect, carelessness or inadvertence'. Note 170 A.L.R. 706; 34 Am. Jur. 631-2; Danielson vs. Roberts, 44 Ore. 108, 74 Pac. 913, . . ."

Citing the same authorities, the court defined mislaid property as:

". . . Property which the owner intentionally places where he can again resort to it, and then forgets. Mislaid property is presumed to be left in the custody of the owner or occupier of the premises upon which it is found, and it is generally held that the right of possession to mislaid property as against all except the owner is in the owner or occupant of such premises."

The court then goes on to state at page 336:

"The facts of this case show that the bills were carefully placed in the jar and then buried in the ground, and further show that the owner did not part with them inadvertently, involuntarily, carelessly or through neglect. Rather it shows a deliberate, conscious and voluntary act of the owner desiring to hide his money in a place where he thought it was safe and secure, and with the intention of returning to claim it at some future date . . . . A lapse of four years was not sufficient to establish that the property had been lost beyond the possibility of restitution to the true owner."

Furthermore, the court in *Hill vs. Schrunk,* supra, held that recent U. S. currency, folded in wax paper which was then folded in oil paper, sealed

237

in a jar, placed in a sealed wooden cask, and then enclosed in a section of an inner tube secured to the bottom of a pool of water, was not abandoned or lost property or treasure trove but was mislaid property because of the care taken to protect it. Also, the court in *Jackson vs. Steinberg,* supra, held that $800.00 neatly folded inside a drawer by the immediately preceding hotel guest was not abandoned or lost property but was mislaid property. If the theory of these cases is applied to our fact situation, the government might contend that because this bullion was so carefully placed in the cave it is mislaid property rather than treasure trove or lost property. However, that argument seems tenuous. In the first place, all of these cases just cited involved paper currency rather than gold. In the second place, they all involved money which had been hidden only a short time as opposed to the extended time during which our bullion was hidden and lost beyond the complete knowledge of any living person. Furthermore, all of these cases involved controversies between the finder and the landowner, which made the characterization of the property very important, while our case is a controversy between two finders, which renders the characterization unimportant. Finally, even if the bullion be classified as mislaid property, the possessory and ownership rights would, nevertheless, seem to belong to Mrs. Noss, since the State of New Mexico has granted her permits for excavating the bullion from state land.

IX. CONCLUSION.

Although there may be some initial concern whether the English and American rules of treasure trove apply to New Mexico, this may be of little consequence in our situation, for the major importance of the other alternatives involves the relative rights of the finder and the landowner, while our case involves the relative rights of the finder and the subsequent finder. Therefore, it probably makes little difference whether the court calls the bullion mislaid property, lost property or treasure trove, although it would probably ease pains of explanation if the court were to adopt the latter classification in this case. The crucial problem is whether Mrs. Noss is a finder either by right of representation or in her own right. Under the facts and the holding of the *Brazelton* case, it would appear that Mrs. Noss has exercised the best control and possession possible under the "salvage" circumstances; at one time Dr. Noss had complete possession, and at all times up until 1952 she was located over the bullion and was in possession and control of the access channel.

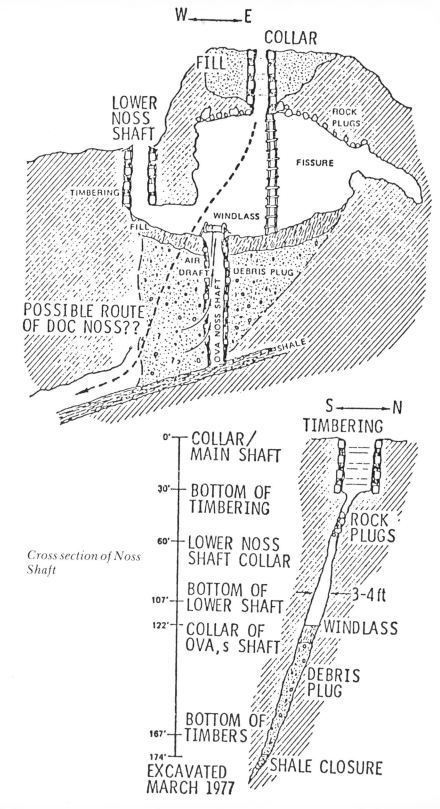

W → E

COLLAR

FILL

LOWER
NOSS
SHAFT

ROCK
PLUGS

TIMBERING

FISSURE

FILL

WINDLASS

AIR
DRAFT

DEBRIS PLUG

POSSIBLE ROUTE
OF DOC NOSS??

OVA NOSS SHAFT

SHALE

S → N

TIMBERING

*Cross section of Noss
Shaft*

0' —	COLLAR/ MAIN SHAFT
30' —	BOTTOM OF TIMBERING
60' —	LOWER NOSS SHAFT COLLAR
107' —	BOTTOM OF LOWER SHAFT
122' —	COLLAR OF OVA,s SHAFT
167' —	BOTTOM OF TIMBERS
174' —	

EXCAVATED
MARCH 1977

ROCK
PLUGS

3-4 ft

WINDLASS

DEBRIS
PLUG

SHALE CLOSURE

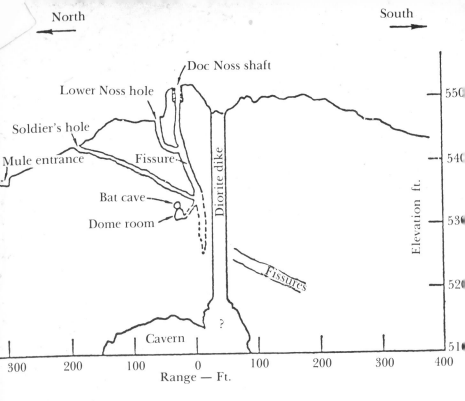

North

South

Doc Noss shaft

Lower Noss hole

Soldier's hole

Mule entrance

Fissure

Bat cave

Dome room

Diorite dike

Fissures

Cavern

?

Elevation — ft.

550
540
530
520
510

300   200   100   0   100   200   300   400

Range — Ft.

North-South cross section of Victoria Peak

VICTORIA PEAK

SHAFT OPEN TO THIS POINT

180

STEPS CUT IN SHAFT WALL

ROCK CAVE-IN

140

Jack Abshier

A Kansas City Star artist's concept of the access of the treasure caverns.